What People Are Saying Threshold Bible Study

"Threshold Bible Study connects the wisdom of God's word to our daily lives. This fine series will provide needed tools that can deepen your understanding of Scripture, but most importantly it can deepen your faith. In the classical tradition of *lectio divina*, this series also offers a very practical way to pray with Scripture, and I can think of nothing better for equipping people for the New Evangelization than a biblically soaked life of prayer."

Most Reverend Charles J. Chaput, O.F.M. Cap., Archbishop of Denver

"Stephen Binz's Threshold Bible Study is a marvelous project. With lucidity and creativity, Binz offers today's believing communities a rich and accessible treasury of biblical scholarship. The series' brilliance lies in its simplicity of presentation complemented by critical depth of thought and reflective insight. This is a wonderful gift for personal and communal study, especially for those wishing to make a home for the word in their hearts."

Carol J. Dempsey, OP, Associate Professor of Theology
University of Portland, OR

"Threshold Bible Study successfully bridges the painful gap between solid biblical scholarship and the rich spiritual nourishment that we expect to find in the words of Scripture. In this way, indispensable biblical knowledge leads to that spiritual wisdom which enables us to live in accord with God's purposes. Stephen Binz is to be congratulated for responding to this urgent need in today's world."

Demetrius Dumm, O.S.B.
Professor of New Testament, Saint Vincent Seminary
Saint Vincent Archabbey, Latrobe, Pennsylvania

"The Church has called Scripture a 'font' and 'wellspring' for the spiritual life. Threshold Bible Study is one of the best sources for tapping into the biblical font. Pope John Paul II has stressed that 'listening to the word of God should become a life-giving encounter.' This is precisely what Threshold Bible Study offers to you—an encounter with the word that will make your heart come alive."

Tim Gray
Director of the Denver Catholic Biblical School

"Threshold Bible Study offers solid scholarship and spiritual depth. Drawing on the Church's living Tradition and the Jewish roots of the New Testament, Threshold Bible Study can be counted on for lively individual study and prayer, even while it offers spiritual riches to deepen communal conversation and reflection among the people of God."

Scott Hahn, Professor of Biblical Theology, Franciscan University of Steubenville

"Stephen Binz offers an invaluable guide that can make reading the Bible enjoyable (again) and truly nourishing. A real education on how to read the Bible, this series prepares people to discuss Scripture and to share it in community."

Jacques Nieuviarts, Professor of Scripture, Institut Catholique de Toulouse, France

"I most strongly recommend Stephen Binz's Threshold Bible Study for adult Bible classes, religious education, and personal spiritual enrichment. The series is exceptional for its scholarly solidity, pastoral practicality, and clarity of presentation. The church owes Binz a great debt of gratitude for his generous and competent labor in the service of the Word of God."   Peter C. Phan, The Ignacio Ellacuria Professor of Catholic Social Thought

Georgetown University

"Threshold Bible Study is an enriching and enlightening approach to understanding the rich faith which the Scriptures hold for us today. Written in a clear and concise style, Threshold Bible Study presents solid contemporary biblical scholarship, offers questions for reflection and/or discussion, and then demonstrates a way to pray from the Scriptures. All these elements work together to offer the reader a wonderful insight into how the sacred texts of our faith can touch our lives in a profound and practical way today. I heartily recommend this series to both individuals and to Bible study groups."

Abbot Gregory J. Polan, O.S.B., Conception Abbey and Seminary College

"Threshold Bible Study helpfully introduces the lay reader into the life-enhancing process of *lectio divina* or prayerful reading of Scripture, individually or in a group. This series, prepared by a reputable biblical scholar and teacher, responds creatively to the exhortation of the Council to provide God' people abundant nourishment from the table of God's word. The process proposed leads the reader from Bible study to personal prayer, community involvement, and active Christian commitment in the world."

Sandra M. Schneiders, Professor of New Testament and Spirituality

Jesuit School of Theology, Berkeley

"Stephen Binz has put together a great aid in one of the most important aspects of Catholic Christian life today: Bible study. Largely the purview for non Catholic Christian laity in the past, recent years have seen Catholic hungering for scripture study and application in their daily lives. Stephen Binz's series promises to help meet that need."

John Michael Talbot, Catholic Christian Recording Artist

Founder of The Brothers and Sisters of Charity at Little Portion Hermitage

"Threshold Bible Study unlocks the Scriptures and ushers the reader over the threshold into the world of God's living word. The world of the Bible comes alive with new meaning and understanding for our times. This series enables the reader to appreciate contemporary biblical scholarship and the meaning of God's word. This is the best material I have seen for serious Bible study."   Most Reverend Donald W. Trautman, Bishop of Erie

The Sacred Heart
of Jesus

Stephen J. Binz

TWENTY
THIRD 23rd
PUBLICATIONS

Twenty-Third Publications
A Division of Bayard
One Montauk Avenue, Suite 200
PO Box 6015
New London, CT 06320
(860)437-3012 or (800) 321-0411
www.23rdpublications.com

ISBN-10: 1-58595-597-3
ISBN 978-1-58595-597-8
Library of Congress Catalog Card Number: 2006902488

Contents

LESSONS 13–18

LESSONS 19–24

LESSONS 25–30

How to Use
Threshold Bible Study

Each book in the Threshold Bible Study series is designed to lead you through a new doorway of biblical awareness, to accompany you across a unique threshold of understanding. The characters, places, and images that you encounter in each of these topical studies will help you explore fresh dimensions of your faith and discover richer insights for your spiritual life.

Threshold Bible Study covers biblical themes in depth in a short amount of time. Unlike more traditional Bible studies that treat a biblical book or series of books, Threshold Bible Study aims to address specific topics within the entire Bible. The goal is not for you to comprehend everything about each passage, but rather for you to understand what a variety of passages from different books of the Bible reveals about the topic of each study.

Threshold Bible Study offers you an opportunity to explore the entire Bible from the viewpoint of a variety of different themes. The commentary that follows each biblical passage launches your reflection about that passage and helps you begin to see its significance within the context of your contemporary experience. The questions following the commentary challenge you to understand the passage more fully and apply it to your own life. The prayer starter helps conclude your study by integrating learning into your relationship with God.

These studies are designed for maximum flexibility. Each study is presented in a workbook format, with sections for reading, reflecting, writing, discussing, and praying. Space for writing after each question is ideal for personal study and allows group members to prepare in advance for their discussion. The thirty lessons in each topic may be used by an individual over the period of a month, or by a group for six sessions, with lessons to be studies each week before the next group meeting. These studies are ideal for Bible study groups, small Christian communities, adult faith formation, student groups, Sunday school, neighborhood groups, and family reading, as well as for individual learning.

The method of Threshold Bible Study is rooted in the classical tradition of *lectio divina*, an ancient yet contemporary means for reading the Scriptures reflectively and prayerfully. Reading and interpreting the text (*lectio*) is followed by reflective meditation on its message (*meditatio*). This reading and reflecting flows into prayer from the heart (*oratio* and *contemplatio*).

This ancient method assures us that Bible study is a matter of both the mind and the heart. It is not just an intellectual exercise to learn more and be able to discuss the Bible with others. It is, more importantly, a transforming experience. Reflecting on God's word, guided by the Holy Spirit, illumines the mind with wisdom and stirs the heart with zeal.

Following the personal Bible study, Threshold Bible Study offers a method for extending *lectio divina* into a weekly conversation with a small group. This communal experience will allow participants to enhance their appreciation of the message and build up a spiritual community (*collatio*). The end result will be to increase not only individual faith, but also faithful witness in the context of daily life (*operatio*).

Through the spiritual disciplines of Scripture reading, study, reflection, conversation, and prayer, you will experience God's grace more abundantly as your life is rooted more deeply in Christ. The risen Jesus said: "Listen! I am standing at the door, knocking; if you hear my voice and open the door, I will come in to you and eat with you, and you with me" (Rev 3:20). Listen to the Word of God, open the door, and cross the threshold to an unimaginable dwelling with God!

SUGGESTIONS FOR INDIVIDUAL STUDY

• Make your Bible reading a time of prayer. Ask for God's guidance as your read the Scriptures.

• Try to study daily, or as often as possible according to the circumstances of your life.

• Read the Bible passage carefully, trying to understand both its meaning and its personal application as you read. Some persons find it helpful to read the passage aloud.

• Read the passage in another Bible translation. Each version adds to your understanding of the original text.

• Allow the commentary to help you comprehend and apply the scriptural text. The commentary is only a beginning, not the last word on the meaning of the passage.

• After reflecting on each question, write out your responses. The very act of writing will help you clarify your thoughts, bring new insights, and amplify your understanding.

• As you reflect on your answers, think about how you can live God's word in the context of your daily life.

• Conclude each daily lesson by reading the prayer and continuing with your own prayer from the heart.

• Make sure your reflections and prayers are matters of both the mind and the heart. A true encounter with God's word is always a transforming experience.

• Choose a word or a phrase from the lesson to carry with you throughout the day as a reminder of your encounter with God's life-changing word.

• Share your learning experience with at least one other person whom you trust for additional insights and affirmation. The ideal way to share learning is in a small group that meets regularly.

SUGGESTIONS FOR GROUP STUDY

• Meet regularly; weekly is ideal. Try to be on time and make attendance a high priority for the sake of the group. The average group meets for about an hour.

• Open each session with a prepared prayer, a song, or a reflection. Find some appropriate way to bring the group from the workaday world into a sacred time of graced sharing.

• If you have not been together before, name tags are very helpful as a group begins to become acquainted with the other group members.

• Spend the first session getting acquainted with one another, reading the Introduction aloud, and discussing the questions that follow.

• Appoint a group facilitator to provide guidance to the discussion. The role of facilitator may rotate among members each week. The facilitator simply keeps the discussion on track; each person shares responsibility for the group. There is no need for the facilitator to be a trained teacher.

• Try to study the six lessons on your own during the week. When you have done your own reflection and written your own answers, you will be better prepared to discuss the six scriptural lessons with the group. If you have not had an opportunity to study the passages during the week, meet with the group anyway to share support and insights.

• Participate in the discussion as much as you are able, offering your thoughts, insights, feelings, and decisions. You learn by sharing with others the fruits of your study.

• Be careful not to dominate the discussion. It is important that everyone in the group be offered an equal opportunity to share the results of their work. Try to link what you say to the comments of others so that the group remains on the topic.

• When discussing your own personal thoughts or feelings, use "I" language. Be as personal and honest as appropriate and be very cautious about giving advice to others.

• Listen attentively to the other members of the group so as to learn from their insights. The words of the Bible affect each person in a different way, so a group provides a wealth of understanding for each member.

• Don't fear silence. Silence in a group is as important as silence in personal study. It allows individuals time to listen to the voice of God's Spirit and the opportunity to form their thoughts before they speak.

• Solicit several responses for each question. The thoughts of different people will build on the answers of others and will lead to deeper insights for all.

• Don't fear controversy. Differences of opinions are a sign of a healthy and honest group. If you cannot resolve an issue, continue on, agreeing to disagree. There is probably some truth in each viewpoint.

• Discuss the questions that seem most important for the group. There is no need to cover all the questions in the group session.

• Realize that some questions about the Bible cannot be resolved, even by experts. Don't get stuck on some issue for which there are no clear answers.

• Whatever is said in the group is said in confidence and should be regarded as such.

• Pray as a group in whatever way feels comfortable. Pray for the members of your group throughout the week.

Schedule for group study

Session 1: Introduction   Date: _____

Session 2: Lessons 1–6   Date: _____

Session 3: Lessons 7–12   Date: _____

Session 4: Lessons 13–18   Date: _____

Session 5: Lessons 19–24   Date: _____

Session 6: Lessons 25–30   Date: _____

The Lord does not see as mortals see; they look on the outward appearance, but the Lord looks on the heart. 1 Sam 16:7

The Sacred Heart of Jesus

There is no image that speaks more powerfully of Catholic devotional practice than the Sacred Heart of Jesus. Dedication to the Sacred Heart has a rich history, evident in the countless religious communities, churches, shrines, and religious institutions, and in the iconography, prayers, hymns, and devotional traditions associated with it. Yet, despite this extensive history, few would deny that devotion to the Sacred Heart has suffered cardiac arrest in our times. For many today, attention to the Sacred Heart seems outdated in a church that is biblically grounded and ecumenically conscious. Nevertheless, numerous indications point to a revitalization of the divine heart at the center of the church. If the energetic pulse of this palpable expression of divine love is to be restored, its recovery must be nourished with the healthy diet of sacred Scripture.

The heart of God, the heart of the incarnate Word, and the hearts of God's people are recurrent symbols throughout Scripture. In the biblical writings, the heart is the center of a person, the core of one's inner life and personality. It is the source of one's deepest motivation, decisions, memories, and desires. For this reason, the heart is the place in which a person encounters God, in which God works to cause conversion, enlightenment, and renewed life.

The Sacred Heart is the potent symbol of divine love discovered in human flesh. It is the center of the redemptive love of Christ for the world, the source from which God's grace flows to renew humanity. A biblical spirituality of the heart, freed from sentimentality, can become again a powerful source of renewal for Christ's church. Revitalized and invigorated, the divine heart can become the ecumenical expression of a new movement of justice and charity in the world, of a new civilization of love.

Reflection and discussion

• What is attractive to me about the image of the Sacred Heart? Why is it such an ideal metaphor for divine love?

• Why is the image of the Sacred Heart displayed as both wounded and glorious?

The Heart Is the Center

People are always more fascinated by what is outside themselves than by the unique, creative world within the human heart. But biblical wisdom teaches us that the quality of a person depends on the quality of that person's heart. All of a person's external behavior is determined by this interior center. A human heart can become hardened, remain closed in on itself, and become the heart of a fool. On the other hand, the heart can be the place where we experience joy, gratitude, wisdom, and abundant life. So God takes a special interest in our hearts; it is the part of the person that God alone can see. It is important that we keep watch over our hearts because the formation of our hearts requires attention and listening. As Proverbs says, "Keep your heart with all vigilance, for from it flow the springs of life" (Prov 4:23).

In ancient times, not much was known about the heart as a physical organ. Yet the people of the ancient world knew that the rhythmic beating of the heart coincided with all the functions of life and its cessation meant death. They knew that they could hear and feel the pulsing of the heart, but they also discerned that they could listen to the heart and feel its movements in a far deeper sense. They recognized that the heart was the font from which flowed all the most important aspects of a person's being, including understanding, feeling, and willing. So listening to the heart and feeling its interior movements was critical to self-understanding and truly knowing another.

According to the biblical literature, emotions, moods, and passions come from the heart. The heart can flow with joy, hatred, sincerity, fear, anger, trust, and grief. The psalmist tells his listeners to delight in God, for "he will give you the desires of your heart" (Ps 37:4). The heart is also the seat of human understanding, the repository of wisdom, the storehouse of memories; it considers things carefully, and has depths that are seemingly limitless. The more recent insight of Blaise Pascal conforms to the understanding of the ancients: "The heart has its reasons of which reason knows nothing."

In the Bible, the heart is always the center of a person's relationship with God. It is the heart that speaks to God, that trusts in God, that prays to God, and that receives God's word. As the psalmist sings, "God knows the secrets of the heart" (Ps 44:21). God can give hearts understanding and inspire them to action. Ultimately, only God can truly change the human heart, and genuine conversion of heart awaits the action of God, when God will write his will on human hearts (Jer 31:33) and replace hardened hearts with hearts of flesh (Ezek 36:26). God can open the heart to listen (Acts 16:14), and God can shine his glory into our hearts (2 Cor 4:6). God strengthens our hearts in holiness (1 Thes 3:13), and God's Spirit dwells in our hearts (2 Cor 1:22).

Reflection and discussion

• In what way does the quote by Augustine, "Our hearts are restless until they rest in Thee," express a biblical understanding of the heart?

• What does it mean to really listen to my heart? If I could take my heart away for a few days, what would it want to say to me?

Close to the Heart of God

If every human heart has unique and mysterious depths that only God can know, how much more wondrous must be the divine depths of the heart of Jesus. At the center of his being was his filial love for the Father, an intimate, confident, obedient relationship between Father and Son. John's gospel introduces Jesus as "God the only Son, who is close to the Father's heart" (John 1:18). Jesus surrendered himself freely and joyfully to the will of his Father, and everything he said and did flowed from this self-offering. The words of the psalmist were truly on his lips and in his heart: "I delight to do your will, O my God; your law is within my heart" (Ps 40:8). Jesus was so united with the Father's heart that he knew God's will within his heart and followed it by loving humanity to the utmost.

In sending his Son into the world, God revealed to us the full depth of his love in a definitive way (1 John 4:9–10). Jesus is the incarnation of God's love; teaching, healing, forgiving, and laying down his life with love that couldn't be greater. The infinite, divine love that filled the heart of Jesus was poured out upon all humanity to show the universality of God's love. It is this love that has been "poured into our hearts through the Holy Spirit" (Rom 5:5). The Spirit that had so filled the heart of Jesus has been sent by God "into our hearts" (Gal 4:6) so that we too can be children of the Father and so that we can love with his love.

The New Testament teaches us how to read the prayers of the psalmist as expressions of the heart of Jesus. Frequently prayed on the lips of Jesus, the psalms articulate his trust in the Father, his compassion for humanity, and his intense suffering for our redemption. While suffering on the cross, Jesus cried out in the depth of his being, expressing the agony of his breaking heart: "My heart is like wax; it is melting within my breast" (Ps 22:14). Tormented and at the point of death, Jesus felt the desolation of the psalmist: "Insults have broken my heart, so that I am in despair. I looked for pity, but there was none; and for comforters, but I found none" (Ps 69:20). But the psalms also express the joyful heart of Christ who knows that he will not be left in the place of death: "My heart is glad and my soul rejoices, for you do not give me up to Sheol, or let your faithful one see the Pit" (Ps 16:9–10). Both Peter (Acts 2:31) and Paul (Acts 13:35) quote this psalm as witness to the Lord's resurrection. These and many other verses from Israel's psalms and prophets express the innermost dispositions found in the sacred heart of Israel's Messiah.

Through the centuries, Christians have sought to learn from the heart of Jesus in order to imitate his virtues. Inspired by his invitation, "Learn from me, for I am gentle and humble of heart" (Matt 11:29), his followers have tried to make their hearts like that of Christ. Christians have also realized that God will mold their hearts when they stay close to the heart of Jesus. The beloved disciple of John's gospel offers the model for this intimacy of the heart as he reclines on the breast of Jesus (John 13:23, 25), just as Jesus was always close to the Father's heart (John 1:18).

The renewal of our hearts is ultimately a gift that flows from the heart of Jesus. During the feast in which his fellow Jews remembered the water that flowed from the rock in the wilderness (Exod 17:6) and anticipated the water that would gush from the temple in the final age (Ezek 47), Jesus proclaimed that rivers of living water would flow from his heart (John 7:38). This ancient promise of God was fulfilled at the death of Jesus on the cross. In his hour of glory, the side of Jesus was pierced with a lance, unleashing the saving water and redeeming blood that flowed from his deepest core. From his eternally wounded heart, life-giving graces would flow into the hearts of all those who put their faith in him.

Reflection and discussion

• In what ways did Jesus show us that God's love is infinite and universal?

• How could I use these biblical truths to develop a spirituality of the heart?

The Pierced and Enflamed Heart

The wounded yet glorified heart of Christ is a powerful image that expresses the love of God for us and evokes love of God from us. As the very center of the crucified yet risen Lord, his sacred heart continues eternally to pulse with love for humanity. During his life, he taught us to love as he loved, and at his death, he gave us the grace to love with his love.

Though images of the divine heart of Jesus vary from age to age and from one culture to another, the sacred heart is usually depicted as both pierced and on fire with love. Often ringed with a crown of thorns and flowing with blood and water, the heart is also radiant and flaming. Though Christ is raised and glorious, his wounds remain forever. The flame does not consume the wooden crown or cauterize the wound in his heart. This paradoxical image expresses the nature of Christ's eternal love for us.

In John's gospel, the risen Christ appears to his disciples with the wounds in his hands and his side. He invites Thomas to place his hand in his pierced side (John 20:27). Though Jesus is glorified, the vestiges of his suffering remain eternally. This same reality is expressed with mystical symbolism in the book of Revelation. There the Lamb is depicted in heaven, "standing as if it had been slaughtered" (Rev 5:6). The Lamb of God is both victorious and slain, bearing the glorified marks of sacrifice forever.

God does not take away suffering, failure, and pain from our lives, but he invites us to unite our hearts with his own. In that union of hearts, our sufferings can become redemptive. Our failures can become the means to our growth and our ability to help others who struggle. Our pains can give us deeper compassion and impel us to become healers for others. Our suffering can become the means to unite us more deeply to Christ and transform us into a source of strength and hope for others.

Our secular tendency is to try to deny pain and make suffering go away. But covering up our wounds may deny us their deeper gifts. When we unite our hearts to the heart of Christ, we will know that our suffering is never wasted. Our hurts can be transformed so that they no longer destroy us, but allow us to realize our essential goodness and live our lives in new ways. When we open our lives to this transformation, we are drawing near to the heart of God.

Reflection and discussion

• What is the reason for the contradictory imagery associated with the Sacred Heart?

• In what way does suffering become redemptive? What examples have I experienced?

A Spirituality of the Heart

While there is no specific mention of adoration of the Sacred Heart of Jesus in the biblical period of early Christianity, we find within the Scriptures all the central ideas and images which fostered the devotion to develop in later centuries. Because of "the boundless riches of Christ" (Eph 3:8), God's word continues to unfold its abundance from age to age. In this study, we will explore the heart of God, the heart of Christ, and the hearts of God's people in the Bible in order to come to experience more deeply the divine love that we are privileged to claim.

The Sacred Heart, pierced and flowing with living streams of blood and water, is a threshold inviting us into the experience of divine love. There are living springs within our own hearts that can sometimes get silted. A reflective and prayerful meditation on these Scriptures offers us a rich spirituality of the heart than can renew our lives and revitalize this rich devotion for our contemporary world.

Prayer

Compassionate and merciful God, you have created our hearts to be oriented toward you. Turn my heart to your word and open my heart to share the life of your Son. Renew me with your Holy Spirit and release the springs of life to flow from my heart. Enlighten and encourage me as I read and contemplate your inspired word in these sacred Scriptures. Show me how to make my life a testimony to your love.

SUGGESTIONS FOR FACILITATORS, GROUP SESSION 1

1.If the group is meeting for the first time, or if there are newcomers joining the group, it is helpful to provide nametags.

2. Distribute the books to the members of the group.

3. You may want to ask the participants to introduce themselves and tell the group a bit about themselves.

4. Ask one or more of these introductory questions:

- What drew you to join this group?
- What is your biggest fear in beginning this Bible study?
- How is beginning this study like a "threshold" for you?

5. You may want to pray this prayer as a group:

Come upon us, Holy Spirit, to enlighten and guide us as we begin this study of the Sacred Heart. Our hearts are hesitant, anxious, and fearful as we begin to read the Scriptures. The inspired word has the power to convert our hearts and change our lives. Fill our hearts with desire, trust, and confidence as you shine the light of your truth within us. Motivate us to read the Scriptures and give us a deeper love for God's word each day. Bless us during this session and throughout the coming week with the fire of your love.

6. Read the Introduction aloud, pausing at each question for discussion. Group members may wish to write the insights of the group as each question is discussed. Encourage several members of the group to respond to each question.

7. Don't feel compelled to finish the complete Introduction during the session. It is better to allow sufficient time to talk about the questions raised than to rush to the end. Group members may read any remaining sections on their own after the group meeting.

8. Instruct group members to read the first six lessons on their own during the six days before the next group meeting. They should write out their own answers to the questions as preparation for next week's group discussion.

9. Fill in the date for each group meeting under "Schedule for Group Study."

10. Conclude by praying aloud together the prayer at the end of the Introduction.

You shall love the Lord your God with all your heart, and with all your soul, and with all your might. Keep these words that I am commanding you today in your heart. Deut 6:5–6

God Set His Heart on You

DEUTERONOMY 6:4–9 *⁴Hear, O Israel: The Lord is our God, the Lord alone. ⁵You shall love the Lord your God with all your heart, and with all your soul, and with all your might. ⁶Keep these words that I am commanding you today in your heart. ⁷Recite them to your children and talk about them when you are at home and when you are away, when you lie down and when you rise. ⁸Bind them as a sign on your hand, fix them as an emblem on your forehead, ⁹and write them on the doorposts of your house and on your gates.*

DEUTERONOMY 7:6–11 *⁶For you are a people holy to the Lord your God; the Lord your God has chosen you out of all the peoples on earth to be his people, his treasured possession. ⁷It was not because you were more numerous than any other people that the Lord set his heart on you and chose you—for you were the fewest of all peoples. ⁸It was because the Lord loved you and kept the oath that he swore to your ancestors, that the Lord has brought you out with a mighty hand, and redeemed you from the house of slavery, from the hand of Pharaoh king of Egypt. ⁹Know therefore that the Lord your God is God, the faithful God*

*who maintains covenant loyalty with those who love him and keep his com-
mandments, to a thousand generations,* [10]*and who repays in their own person
those who reject him. He does not delay but repays in their own person those who
reject him.* [11]*Therefore, observe diligently the commandment—the statutes, and
the ordinances—that I am commanding you today.*

The inexplicable love of God for Israel is the foundation of God's saving relationship with his people. God "set his heart" on Israel (7:7),
choosing them out of all the peoples of the earth, simply because he
desired to love them. The words chosen by the author of Deuteronomy to
express God's love suggest a passionate desire and loving commitment. All
peoples belong to God in some sense, yet Israel was specially chosen to be
God's "treasured possession" (7:6). And because Israel held this treasured
place in God's eyes, they were called to be holy to the Lord, living in a sacred
relationship with the God of all nations.

Yet this choice of God to love Israel could never become a source of self-
inflated pride for the Israelites because it was totally undeserved. There was
no special characteristic or attractive attributes in Israel that would evoke
God's love and choice of them. In fact, quite the contrary (7:7). The reason,
then? "It was because the Lord loved you" (7:8). It's as simple and as wonderful as that. This love of God is a faithful, steadfast, and loyal love.

Being the beloved treasure of God has significant implications for Israel's
life. God expects the Israelites to reflect his way with them: the one who loves
his people and keeps the covenant with them expects his people to love him
wholeheartedly and keep the covenant commandments. There is no room for
an apathetic middle ground; they either love God or reject him (7:10). When
Israel responds in love, the opportunities for life are abundant. God's love is
continuous and expansive, "to a thousand generations" (7:9).

The Shema (6:4–5) is the heart of Israel's Torah (the law given through
Moses); it is the hub around which everything else revolves. Named for the
first Hebrew word of the command, "Hear," the Shema is the centerpiece of
Jewish daily worship. It consists of both an affirmation about God and a call
for commitment to God.

The initial function of the Shema (6:4) is to identify the Lord who is the
center and source of Israel's existence as a people. The declaration about God

can be translated in two ways: "the Lord alone" or "the Lord is one." Israel must struggle with the implications of both: the Lord alone is our God and the Lord our God is one. Because God is one and undivided, Israel's love and loyalty must be undivided.

The call of Israel to love God (6:5) is rooted in the God's prior love for them, demonstrated in God's redeeming history with his people. "We love because he first loved us" (1 John 4:19), though a New Testament phrase, expresses the fact that the love God asks of his people is itself God's grace. We are able to love because we have been loved first. This love does not suggest so much an emotional response, but implies a faithful, loyal, and intimate relationship.

This love for God must be wholehearted. The wholeness and oneness of God must be met with a response from the whole, complete human person. "With all your heart" means to love with all your will, intention, and commitment. "With all your soul" means to love with all your passions and desires. "With all your might" adds a superlative degree, indicating that loving God should be "over the top."

If these words are indeed the center of the covenant, then what are God's people to do with them? First and foremost, they must place them in their hearts (6:6). Following the commandments of God was not to be a matter of legalistic conformity to external rules. Loving loyalty was an internal choice of the heart manifested in external actions. A rapid series of verbs helps us feel the urgency of the command: "Keep these words....Recite them...talk about them....Bind them...fix them...write them (6:6–9). Teaching these words to children, talking about these words at all places and throughout the day, these are the ways that God's people flavored the whole of life with conscious attention to God.

Fixing the words on one's forehead and hand (6:8) means binding them into one's own individual life. Writing the words on one's doorposts (6:9) means making them vital for one's home and family. Inscribing them on the city gates (6:9), the place of public business and civic life, means making them crucial for society. Believers must work out the meaning of loving God in appropriate ways for all three levels. By the time of Jesus, Jews literally placed parchment copies of the Shema in leather (*tefillin*) and tied them to their foreheads and arms, and they affixed encased copies of the Shema to the doors of their homes (*mezuzot*) as external reminders of the heartfelt desire to love God.

Reflection and discussion

• What difference does it make in my life that God has set his heart on me and chose me as his treasured possession?

• In what way does being loved first by God enable me then to love God and other people? Why is it necessary to be loved before being able to love?

• In what way can external religious symbols promote internal attitudes of the heart? Give examples.

Prayer

Creator and Lord, you are the one and only God. Thank you for loving me and choosing me as your treasured possession. Give me a heartfelt love for you. Bestow on me the grace to love you completely in my personal life, my family life, and my communal life.

The Lord set his heart in love on your ancestors alone and chose you, their descendants after them, out of all the peoples, as it is today. Circumcise, then, the foreskin of your heart, and do not be stubborn any longer. Deut 10:15–16

Circumcise Your Heart

DEUTERONOMY 10:12–22 ¹²*So now, O Israel, what does the Lord your God require of you? Only to fear the Lord your God, to walk in all his ways, to love him, to serve the Lord your God with all your heart and with all your soul, ¹³and to keep the commandments of the Lord your God and his decrees that I am commanding you today, for your own well-being. ¹⁴Although heaven and the heaven of heavens belong to the Lord your God, the earth with all that is in it, ¹⁵yet the Lord set his heart in love on your ancestors alone and chose you, their descendants after them, out of all the peoples, as it is today. ¹⁶Circumcise, then, the foreskin of your heart, and do not be stubborn any longer. ¹⁷For the Lord your God is God of gods and Lord of lords, the great God, mighty and awesome, who is not partial and takes no bribe, ¹⁸who executes justice for the orphan and the widow, and who loves the strangers, providing them food and clothing. ¹⁹You shall also love the stranger, for you were strangers in the land of Egypt. ²⁰You shall fear the Lord your God; him alone you shall worship; to him you shall hold fast, and by his name you shall swear. ²¹He is your praise; he is your God, who has done for you these great and awesome things that your own eyes have seen.*

14

²²*Your ancestors went down to Egypt seventy persons; and now the Lord your God has made you as numerous as the stars in heaven.*

What is the appropriate human response to God? In a digest of the Torah, summing up the essence of what God asks of us, the text lists these five actions: to fear the Lord, to walk in all his ways, to love the Lord, to serve him, and to keep his commandments (verses 12–13). All of these flow from the middle and central act—to love God—and all are to be done with one's whole being. This is what it means to live in a covenanted relationship with God.

Again, in summary fashion, the text expresses the wonder of God's choice of Israel. Out of all the other peoples of the world, "the Lord set his heart in love" on their ancestors and their descendants (verse 15). In the previous passage, the marvel was that God should have chosen Israel because they were so small (7:7). Here, the marvel is that God is so great (verse 14). Though he owns the entire cosmos, God still focused his affection on insignificant Israel. In both passages, the message is that God's choice of Israel was based on nothing in themselves that evoked God's favoritism, but solely on the incomprehensible love of God.

The fitting response to God's inconceivable love for his people is expressed in a challenging phrase: "circumcise the foreskin of your heart" (verse 16). Physical circumcision for male Israelites was always a sign of belonging to God and dedication to the covenant. The outward sign expressed an inner orientation, the surrender of one's life to God. Circumcision of the heart is a metaphor that expresses the need to cut away whatever blocks the heart from God's teaching and makes the heart inaccessible to the experience of God's love. A circumcised heart is one that is totally open and dedicated to the Lord. The interior disposition of a person was more important in Israel's relationship with God than any external practice.

Paul writes about this circumcision of the heart in his letter to the Romans: "Real circumcision is a matter of the heart—it is spiritual and not literal" (Rom 2:29). He is arguing that the uncircumcised Gentiles are capable of following in God's ways because being God's people is not a matter of external and physical marks. It is an inner reality perceived not by other people but by God.

A thick and hardened heart is the major obstacle that prevents us from experiencing the fullness of life that God wants for his people. It was Pharaoh's hardened heart that kept the Israelites enslaved in Egypt (Exod 7:13), and Israel's resistance to God's direction in the wilderness was evidence of their hardness of heart (Ps 95:8). The Israelites are warned against becoming hard-hearted: "Do not become hard-hearted or tight-fisted toward your needy neighbor" (Deut 15:7). The heart that God desires in us is one that is open to God as well as to people in need.

Reflection and discussion

• Compare the summary of the law (Deut 10:12–13) with the summary of the prophets (Micah 6:8). What is similar and what is different between the law and the prophets?

• God loved Israel simply because he chose to, not because Israel deserved his love. How is this quality of love echoed in God's command for Israel to love the stranger (foreigner) in their land (verse 19)?

• Why did God use the image of circumcision as a metaphor for the type of heart he desires in us?

• How does Paul explain the meaning of the circumcised heart (Rom 2:29)?

• What is hard-heartedness? When do I sense myself becoming hard-hearted?

Prayer

God of gods and Lord of lords, you are mighty and awesome, yet you set your heart in love upon Israel. Open my stubborn heart to people in need. Help me to care for the orphan and the widow, to love the foreigner, and to love without expecting return.

The Lord your God will circumcise your heart and the heart of your descendants, so that you will love the Lord your God with all your heart and with all your soul, in order that you may live. Deut 30:6

Turn to the Lord with Your Whole Heart

DEUTERONOMY 30:1–20 ¹*When all these things have happened to you, the blessings and the curses that I have set before you, if you call them to mind among all the nations where the Lord your God has driven you, ²and return to the Lord your God, and you and your children obey him with all your heart and with all your soul, just as I am commanding you today, ³then the Lord your God will restore your fortunes and have compassion on you, gathering you again from all the peoples among whom the Lord your God has scattered you. ⁴Even if you are exiled to the ends of the world, from there the Lord your God will gather you, and from there he will bring you back. ⁵The Lord your God will bring you into the land that your ancestors possessed, and you will possess it; he will make you more prosperous and numerous than your ancestors.*

⁶Moreover, the Lord your God will circumcise your heart and the heart of your descendants, so that you will love the Lord your God with all your heart and with all your soul, in order that you may live. ⁷The Lord your God will put all these curses on your enemies and on the adversaries who took advantage of you.

⁸*Then you shall again obey the Lord, observing all his commandments that I am commanding you today, ⁹and the Lord your God will make you abundantly prosperous in all your undertakings, in the fruit of your body, in the fruit of your livestock, and in the fruit of your soil. For the Lord will again take delight in prospering you, just as he delighted in prospering your ancestors, ¹⁰when you obey the Lord your God by observing his commandments and decrees that are written in this book of the law, because you turn to the Lord your God with all your heart and with all your soul.*

¹¹*Surely, this commandment that I am commanding you today is not too hard for you, nor is it too far away. ¹²It is not in heaven, that you should say, "Who will go up to heaven for us, and get it for us so that we may hear it and observe it?" ¹³Neither is it beyond the sea, that you should say, "Who will cross to the other side of the sea for us, and get it for us so that we may hear it and observe it?" ¹⁴No, the word is very near to you; it is in your mouth and in your heart for you to observe.*

¹⁵*See, I have set before you today life and prosperity, death and adversity. ¹⁶If you obey the commandments of the Lord your God that I am commanding you today, by loving the Lord your God, walking in his ways, and observing his commandments, decrees, and ordinances, then you shall live and become numerous, and the Lord your God will bless you in the land that you are entering to possess. ¹⁷But if your heart turns away and you do not hear, but are led astray to bow down to other gods and serve them, ¹⁸I declare to you today that you shall perish; you shall not live long in the land that you are crossing the Jordan to enter and possess. ¹⁹I call heaven and earth to witness against you today that I have set before you life and death, blessings and curses. Choose life so that you and your descendants may live, ²⁰loving the Lord your God, obeying him, and holding fast to him; for that means life to you and length of days, so that you may live in the land that the Lord swore to give to your ancestors, to Abraham, to Isaac, and to Jacob.*

This exhortation to choose God's way and renew the covenant occurs when Israel is on the border of the promised land and about to cross over to claim God's promises. Yet, it also envisions a time much later when God's people would be exiled far and wide among other nations (verse 4). God promises to have compassion on them, bring them back, and make them prosperous again with the blessings of the covenant (verses 3, 5). Since the covenant must be renewed in every generation, Israel created liturgies of covenant renewal in which the people would listen to the words of Deuteronomy and then make a decision. The choice is life or death, blessings or curses (verse 19). The decision is not recorded here; it is up to each generation and each person who reads God's word to make that choice.

The choice that is set before Israel can only be made because God has already chosen them and drawn them into covenant by all he has done in their behalf. Because they have experienced God's guidance and care for them in the desert, they can now claim God's way as their own by renewing their covenant with God. In the wilderness without power and wealth, they have come to know God, the loving source of all their gifts. They now know that their ability to live in covenant with God is a continuation of God's grace toward them.

Israel's wholehearted return to the Lord (verse 2) interweaves both divine and human action. It occurs with Israel's turning and rededication to God. But that conversion cannot happen apart from God's decision to circumcise their hearts so that they can love God wholeheartedly (verse 6). Conversion of the heart is, on the one hand, a decision and commitment to direct one's life toward the will of God and, on the other hand, an accomplishment of the gracious power of God at work within the person. The fundamental commandment—to love God with all one's heart and soul—is ultimately the fruit of God's grace at work within the human heart.

What God asks of his people is described as a single commandment (verse 11), the center of the Torah, a faithful, wholehearted, committed love of God. It is a commandment that is "not too hard" nor "too far away"; that is, God's command is not too complicated, idealistic, or impractical to be practiced by ordinary people. God's will is such that all people are capable of living a life that is faithful and pleasing to God. This truth is powerfully, yet simply expressed in the text's description of the closeness of God's word: "The word is very near to you; it is in your mouth and in your heart for you to observe" (verse 14). God's people are capable of turning to God and following the commandment to love because God has already prepared their hearts and planted his word there.

Reflection and discussion

• Why is the choice posed in verse 19 made with such passionate emotion, energy, and urgency—as a life-or-death choice?

• Compare 10:16 with 30:6. Why is conversion of the heart described as both a human work and the action of God?

• What practical consequences for my life are implied by the encouraging words of verses 11–14?

Prayer

Faithful and loving God, you have given us your commandment to love and shown us your will for our lives in a way that is accessible to all people. Thank you for placing your word in my heart and for giving me the grace to always choose the way of life, blessings, and love.

This is the covenant that I will make with the house of Israel after those days, says the Lord: I will put my law within them, and I will write it on their hearts; and I will be their God, and they shall be my people. Jer 31:33

Promise of the New Covenant

JEREMIAH 31:31–34 ³¹*The days are surely coming, says the Lord, when I will make a new covenant with the house of Israel and the house of Judah.* ³²*It will not be like the covenant that I made with their ancestors when I took them by the hand to bring them out of the land of Egypt—a covenant that they broke, though I was their husband, says the Lord.* ³³*But this is the covenant that I will make with the house of Israel after those days, says the Lord: I will put my law within them, and I will write it on their hearts; and I will be their God, and they shall be my people.* ³⁴*No longer shall they teach one another, or say to each other, "Know the Lord," for they shall all know me, from the least of them to the greatest, says the Lord; for I will forgive their iniquity, and remember their sin no more.*

Jeremiah's prophecy is the one place in the Old Testament in which a new covenant is proclaimed. This new covenant between God and his people would be qualitatively different from the covenant God made with the Israelites at Mount Sinai after he brought them forth from the slavery of Egypt (Exod 19–24). That covenant had been broken by Israel, even though God was Israel's "husband" (verse 32).

What happens after someone breaks a marriage covenant depends entirely on what the two partners do next. Will the wronged partner bring an end to the relationship, do the spouses agree to go on as if nothing happened, or could the spouse possibly forgive what has been done and begin the covenant again on new grounds? Without denying the grievous nature of the wrong or the inevitable consequences of the betrayal, the unfathomably merciful Lord of Israel decides: "I will forgive their iniquity, and remember their sin no more" (verse 34).

This covenant is not something completely different from the covenant formed at Sinai. The first covenant is not annulled: God would still be Israel's God and Israel would be God's people (verse 33). What is new about this covenant that God will make with his people in the future? It is the way in which God will give his Torah to his people: "I will put my law within them, and I will write it on their hearts." In the Sinai covenant God wrote his Torah on tablets of stone. Israel had to learn it in order to know God and know how to live. But in the new covenant, God writes the Torah on their hearts.

Israel had broken the former covenant because their hearts had become hardened against God's law and they refused to change. Their sin was written indelibly on their hearts. As Jeremiah explained: "The sin of Judah is written with an iron pen; with a diamond point it is engraved on the tablet of their hearts" (17:1). But this covenant for the end of the ages will be an unbreakable relationship because it will be based on the rightly-directed heart. Israel will know God and desire God's ways from their inmost selves because God will wondrously change the hearts of his people with his forgiving grace. Here at last are the grounds for an indissoluble marriage with all its delights.

The New Testament teaches that this new covenant has entered the world with Jesus. But have our hearts been transformed in such a way that we instinctively and interiorly know God and follow God's teachings? Do we no longer need to be taught God's law? Do we now have nothing of which we need to repent? Clearly Jeremiah's prophecy has not been fulfilled in our hearts.

Yet, there is one heart that knows God completely. There is one heart on which God's Torah has been written so that it is obeyed with the greatest desire in full freedom. It is the heart of Jesus. In this heart we find the first and perfect realization of the new covenant, and in this heart the new covenant has come to Israel. In Jesus, the son of Abraham from the house of Israel and Judah, the ancient promise is fulfilled. From his heart, all the children of Abraham, indeed all of humanity, can live in faith as we await the day when all people, "from the least of them to the greatest" (verse 34), will know the Lord.

Reflection and discussion

• What is the same and what is different about the old covenant and the new covenant?

• Is it possible for people to forgive as God forgives (verse 34)? What does forgiveness do for the human heart?

• Why is God called the "husband" of Israel? What does it mean for God's people to be the bride and wife of God?

• In what specific ways is Jesus the first and perfect realization of the new covenant?

• In what way has Jeremiah's prophecy been fulfilled? In what way has it not yet been fulfilled?

Prayer

God of Israel, through your prophets you taught your people to await a new covenant, a permanent and intimate bond with you, rooted in the hearts of your people. Help us to live in the heart of your Son by faith, so that we can know you and follow your will with our deepest desire.

A new heart I will give you, and a new spirit I will put within you; and I will remove from your body the heart of stone and give you a heart of flesh.

Ezek 36:26

From Heart of Stone to Heart of Flesh

EZEKIEL 11:14–21 ¹⁴*Then the word of the Lord came to me:* ¹⁵*Mortal, your kinsfolk, your own kin, your fellow exiles, the whole house of Israel, all of them, are those of whom the inhabitants of Jerusalem have said, "They have gone far from the Lord; to us this land is given for a possession."* ¹⁶*Therefore say: Thus says the Lord God: Though I removed them far away among the nations, and though I scattered them among the countries, yet I have been a sanctuary to them for a little while in the countries where they have gone.* ¹⁷*Therefore say: Thus says the Lord God: I will gather you from the peoples, and assemble you out of the countries where you have been scattered, and I will give you the land of Israel.* ¹⁸*When they come there, they will remove from it all its detestable things and all its abominations.* ¹⁹*I will give them one heart, and put a new spirit within them; I will remove the heart of stone from their flesh and give them a heart of flesh,* ²⁰*so that they may follow my statutes and keep my ordinances and obey them. Then they shall be my people, and I will be their God.* ²¹*But as for those whose heart goes after their detestable things and their abominations, I will bring their deeds upon their own heads, says the Lord God.*

EZEKIEL 36:22–32   *²²Therefore say to the house of Israel, Thus says the Lord God: It is not for your sake, O house of Israel, that I am about to act, but for the sake of my holy name, which you have profaned among the nations to which you came. ²³I will sanctify my great name, which has been profaned among the nations, and which you have profaned among them; and the nations shall know that I am the Lord, says the Lord God, when through you I display my holiness before their eyes. ²⁴I will take you from the nations, and gather you from all the countries, and bring you into your own land.*

²⁵I will sprinkle clean water upon you, and you shall be clean from all your uncleannesses, and from all your idols I will cleanse you. ²⁶A new heart I will give you, and a new spirit I will put within you; and I will remove from your body the heart of stone and give you a heart of flesh. ²⁷I will put my spirit within you, and make you follow my statutes and be careful to observe my ordinances. ²⁸Then you shall live in the land that I gave to your ancestors; and you shall be my people, and I will be your God. ²⁹I will save you from all your uncleannesses, and I will summon the grain and make it abundant and lay no famine upon you. ³⁰I will make the fruit of the tree and the produce of the field abundant, so that you may never again suffer the disgrace of famine among the nations. ³¹Then you shall remember your evil ways, and your dealings that were not good; and you shall loathe yourselves for your iniquities and your abominable deeds. ³²It is not for your sake that I will act, says the Lord God; let that be known to you. Be ashamed and dismayed for your ways, O house of Israel.

Ezekiel offered hope to Israel who had been exiled to foreign lands as a consequence of their unfaithful past. Though all the institutions that sustained the covenant with God's people seemed to be destroyed—Jerusalem, its temple, and ritual sacrifice—God promised to restore Israel through an external return to the land and an internal transformation. God's gracious action toward his people in returning them from exile was not done because of any merit on the part of Israel, but for the purpose of sanctifying God's name. Making God's name holy was the driving force of Israel's election as God's people, a concern later voiced by Jesus in the first petition of the Lord's prayer (Matt 6:9). Because God's name had been desecrated and defiled among the nations of the earth because of Israel's infidelity to the covenant, God intended to restore Israel for the sake of his name. As God proclaimed through his prophet, "I will sanctify my great name, which has been profaned among the nations" (36:23).

In restoring his people from their sinful past and harsh exile, God promised to cleanse his people with water (36:25). In Israel's ritual practices, the rite of purification by water marked a person's reentry into the worshiping community. Sprinkling clean water on Israel marked the end of an unfaithful past and the beginning of a new phase of existence. Yet, this external symbol of cleansing from sin would only be effective if it were accompanied by an internal transformation, a change of heart.

This interior renovation of God's people is accomplished through the gift of God's grace. Their failures had been so persistent that they were unable to reform themselves. A new divine initiative was needed to bring God's people to a new level of relationship with God. God promised Israel "a new heart," an inner core that is spiritually alive and receptive to the abundant life God wanted for his people. This new interior life would be driven by "one heart" (11:19), a single-hearted loyalty to God, not a heart divided between God and other gods.

God's action on behalf of his people is described as a heart transplant: "I will remove from your body the heart of stone and give you a heart of flesh" (11:19; 36:26). This dramatic spiritual transformation occurs through the inconceivable skill of the divine surgeon. The hardened, stony heart, now totally ineffective because of Israel's chronically unhealthy lifestyle, is replaced by a pliable, healthy heart, capable of beating to the rhythms of God's heartbeat. This "heart of flesh" is responsive to God's will and open to the love of God and neighbor stipulated by God's Torah.

Though the conversion of God's people begins with the heart, it must be accompanied by a transfusion of God's spirit. The desire to do God's will can only be sustained when the "new spirit" also pulses through God's people. Through God's gift of the new heart and the new spirit, the "new covenant" promised in the words of Jeremiah can become a reality. On that day, God proclaims, "you shall be my people, and I will be your God" (11:20; 36:28).

Reflection and discussion

• What would be the diagnosis if the divine physician were to examine my heart today?

• What does the image of the heart transplant tell me about what God wants for his people?

• Why must the heart transplant be accompanied by a transfusion of God's spirit? In what way does the work of Jesus fulfill these promises of Ezekiel's prophecy?

Prayer

Divine Physician, you replace the stony heart of your people with a heart of flesh. Thank you for the inner transformation you give to me through the love of your Son, Jesus. Help me to respond to you like Jesus and to love as he loved. Make my heart like his, for the glory of your holy name.

My heart recoils within me; my compassion grows warm and tender.
I will not execute my fierce anger. Hos 11:8–9

God's Compassionate Love for Israel

HOSEA 11:1–11

¹ *When Israel was a child, I loved him,*
and out of Egypt I called my son.
² *The more I called them,*
the more they went from me;
they kept sacrificing to the Baals,
and offering incense to idols.

³ *Yet it was I who taught Ephraim to walk,*
I took them up in my arms;
but they did not know that I healed them.
⁴ *I led them with cords of human kindness,*
with bands of love.
I was to them like those
who lift infants to their cheeks.
I bent down to them and fed them.

⁵*They shall return to the land of Egypt,*
  and Assyria shall be their king,
  because they have refused to return to me.
⁶*The sword rages in their cities,*
  it consumes their oracle-priests,
  and devours because of their schemes.
⁷*My people are bent on turning away from me.*
  To the Most High they call,
  but he does not raise them up at all.

⁸ *How can I give you up, Ephraim?*
  How can I hand you over, O Israel?
How can I make you like Admah?
  How can I treat you like Zeboiim?
My heart recoils within me;
  my compassion grows warm and tender.
⁹*I will not execute my fierce anger;*
  I will not again destroy Ephraim;
for I am God and no mortal,
  the Holy One in your midst,
  and I will not come in wrath.

¹⁰*They shall go after the Lord,*
  who roars like a lion;
when he roars,
  his children shall come trembling from the west.
¹¹*They shall come trembling like birds from Egypt,*
  and like doves from the land of Assyria;
  and I will return them to their homes, says the Lord.

Few passages of the Bible express God's compassionate love for his people more wonderfully than this oracle of the prophet Hosea. The relationship between God and his people is described as that of a parent and child. God adopted Israel as his "son" in the exodus from Egypt (verse 1). Israel did nothing to deserve this love; God simply "set his heart" on Israel and chose them (Deut 7:6–8). Hosea expresses the covenant relationship formed by God with his people in terms of the deep devotion of a parent for a child.

God expresses his tender love for Israel (Ephraim is another word for the northern kingdom of Israel) through a series of "I" statements: I loved, I called, I taught, I healed, I led, I fed (verses 1–4). The images of parental affection indicate the closeness of God to Israel. God was with Israel from infancy, patiently teaching them to walk, leading them with each new step along the way, taking them in his arms when they fell. God bent down to be with his people, feeding them and lifting them up like parents who lift their infants to their cheeks.

Yet despite all this undeserved love, Israel continually turned away from God and worshiped other gods (verse 2). God expresses here the conflicting emotions of a parent whose child has rebelled. God's love is tender but tough. There comes a time when discipline must be used, when punishment is necessary. Israel will experience a new captivity as in Egypt; they will be ruled by Assyria (verses 5–6). Their enemies will destroy their cities, slaughter their priests, and demolish the places where they offered sacrifices to other gods. Yet no amount of stubborn rebellion can terminate God's lasting love for his children.

Hosea gives us a rare view of the suffering heart of God (verse 8). As God contemplates the captivity and ruin of his people, he cannot stand the thought of it. God cannot let them be destroyed like the other cities (Admah and Zeboiim, Deut 29:23). God breaks out in grief and sobbing at the idea of giving away his beloved child: "My heart recoils within me; my compassion grows warm and tender." The repeated "I will not," "I will not," "I will not," expresses God's adamant refusal to surrender his children to everlasting destruction (verse 9). For God is "the Holy One," whose inexhaustible love is qualitatively different from that of mortals. Even though Israel's response is totally faithless, God cannot give up his child.

God's fierce love will roar like a lion, God's children will eventually come back to him, and God will return them to their homes (verses 10–11). No amount of rebellion will overcome the love of God, who wants to save his children and give them a future. God's love for his adopted son, Israel, is completed in God's love for his begotten Son, Jesus. God's words to his infant son Israel, "Out of Egypt I have called my son" (verse 1), are used by Matthew's gospel to express God's compassion for his newborn Son, Jesus (Matt 2:15). The stony and rebellious heart of his people will be replaced by the new and obedient heart of Jesus. Through his heart all God's children will return home to experience the relentless and everlasting love of God.

Reflection and discussion

• At what age are children most endearing? To which feelings of God can parents most relate?

• Which quality of a parent have I most often experienced from God? In what way is genuine love both tender and tough?

• What does verses 8–9 add to my understanding of the heart of God?

Prayer

Holy One, your love for your children is relentless and everlasting. Despite the destruction and bondage that our rebellion causes us, you continue to give us hope in the life you promise. Through the heart of your Son, lead us to repentance and bring us home to live with you.

SUGGESTIONS FOR FACILITATORS, GROUP SESSION 2

1. If there are newcomers who were not present for the first group session, introduce them now.

2. You may want to pray this prayer as a group:

Holy and merciful God, your love for your people is far beyond what we can expect or understand. You have set your heart upon us and chose us as your treasured possession. Yet, our hearts become hardened and resistant to you and to our neighbor. Give us pliable, healthy hearts, capable of pulsing with the rhythms of your heart. As we study the Scriptures of your covenant, place your word within us and write it on our hearts, so that we will freely choose the way of life that you desire for us.

3. Ask one or more of the following questions:

- What was your biggest challenge in Bible study over this past week?
- What did you learn about yourself this week?

4. Discuss lessons 1 through 6 together. Assuming that group members have read the Scripture and commentary during the week, there is no need to read it aloud. As you review each lesson, you might want to briefly summarize the Scripture passages of each lesson and ask the group what stands out most clearly from the commentary.

5. Choose one or more of the questions for reflection and discussion from each lesson to talk over as a group. You may want to ask group members which question was most challenging or helpful to them as you review each lesson.

6. Keep the discussion moving, but don't rush the discussion in order to complete more questions. Allow time for the questions that provoke the most discussion.

7. Instruct group members to complete lessons 7 through 12 on their own during the six days before the next group meeting. They should write out their own answers to the questions as preparation for next week's group discussion.

8. Conclude by praying aloud together the prayer at the end of lesson 6, or any other prayer you choose.

They drank from the spiritual rock that followed them, and the rock was Christ. 1 Cor 10:4

Abundant Water from the Rock

EXODUS 17:1–7 ¹*From the wilderness of Sin the whole congregation of the Israelites journeyed by stages, as the Lord commanded. They camped at Rephidim, but there was no water for the people to drink.* ²*The people quarreled with Moses, and said, "Give us water to drink." Moses said to them, "Why do you quarrel with me? Why do you test the Lord?"* ³*But the people thirsted there for water; and the people complained against Moses and said, "Why did you bring us out of Egypt, to kill us and our children and livestock with thirst?"* ⁴*So Moses cried out to the Lord, "What shall I do with this people? They are almost ready to stone me."* ⁵*The Lord said to Moses, "Go on ahead of the people, and take some of the elders of Israel with you; take in your hand the staff with which you struck the Nile, and go.* ⁶*I will be standing there in front of you on the rock at Horeb. Strike the rock, and water will come out of it, so that the people may drink." Moses did so, in the sight of the elders of Israel.* ⁷*He called the place Massah and Meribah, because the Israelites quarreled and tested the Lord, saying, "Is the Lord among us or not?"*

NUMBERS 20:7–11 *[7]The Lord spoke to Moses, saying: [8]Take the staff, and assemble the congregation, you and your brother Aaron, and command the rock before their eyes to yield its water. Thus you shall bring water out of the rock for them; thus you shall provide drink for the congregation and their livestock. [9]So Moses took the staff from before the Lord, as he had commanded him. [10]Moses and Aaron gathered the assembly together before the rock, and he said to them, "Listen, you rebels, shall we bring water for you out of this rock?" [11]Then Moses lifted up his hand and struck the rock twice with his staff; water came out abundantly, and the congregation and their livestock drank.*

Traveling through the desert was a time of harsh testing for the Israelites, but it also helped them learn to trust. In this way their sojourn in the wilderness became an image for the journey of faith. The Israelites were led by God through a land that had no signposts. They began to regret their freedom and long for the days of their bondage in Egypt. God's people wondered whether God was really present with them or not. While complaining that they had no water, they tested God by asking for a concrete sign of his care.

The wilderness is not the place God desired for his people's dwelling. God wants his people to live in a land flowing with water abundantly. Yet, in a land where water is scarce, the gifts of God are even more evident. God gave instructions to Moses on how to find water for his people: "Strike the rock, and water will come out of it, so that the people may drink" (Exod 17:6). In the midst of harsh suffering, God provided life-giving water for Israel to drink. Exodus and Numbers give two stories of God's gift of water from the rock, one before God's gift of the Torah at Sinai and one after. Jewish rabbinical tradition held that the rock followed Israel in its travels through the desert as the constant source of refreshing water.

The wilderness account of the rock and its life-giving water provided images for early Christian reflection on Jesus, the gift of his Spirit, and the waters of baptism. When read in the light of the risen Christ, New Testament authors understood these accounts as foreshadowing the abundant life God would give to the church through the suffering and death of his Son. In his letter to the Corinthians, Paul writes that the rock in the wilderness is Christ:

"They drank from the spiritual rock that followed them, and the rock was Christ" (1 Cor 10:4).

The people of Israel remembered their sojourn in the wilderness every year with the festival of Tabernacles. As part of their celebration, each day the priest would carry a golden pitcher of water to the temple and solemnly pour it out over the altar of sacrifice while the people sang the words of Isaiah, "With joy you will draw water from the wells of salvation" (Isa 12:3). This liturgical action was a commemoration of God's providence to their ancestors in the wilderness as he brought forth gushing water from the rock. John's gospel narrates that Jesus attended this festival at the temple and cried out, "Let anyone who is thirsty come to me, and let the one who believes in me drink. As the Scripture has said, 'Out of his heart shall flow rivers of living water'" (John 7:37–38). Jesus is the rock from which the living waters flow. In his saving death, streams of water will flow out from within him to be the source of life and grace for the world.

Reflection and discussion

• When have I been the thirstiest? Why is water such an effective symbol of God's life and blessings?

• In what ways is Israel's journey through the wilderness an image for the consolations and desolations of the spiritual life?

• What was God teaching his people in the wilderness through the gift of water from the rock? What is the lesson for me?

• How did the Jewish people commemorate God's gift of water in the wilderness? Why was it important to remember that gift?

• In what ways do New Testament writers demonstrate that the water from the rock foreshadows the gifts that Christ would bring?

Prayer

Lord God, you gave your people water from the rock in the wilderness. Help me to trust in you and to realize that you are my source of life and blessings. Refresh me with the living waters of your Spirit that flow from the heart of your Son.

With joy you will draw water from the wells of salvation. And you will say in that day: Give thanks to the Lord, call on his name; make known his deeds among the nations; proclaim that his name is exalted. Isa 12:3–4

Drawing Water from Salvation's Font

ISAIAH 12:1–6

[1] *You will say in that day:*
I will give thanks to you, O Lord,
   for though you were angry with me,
your anger turned away,
   and you comforted me.

[2] *Surely God is my salvation;*
   I will trust, and will not be afraid,
for the Lord God is my strength and my might;
   he has become my salvation.

[3] *With joy you will draw water from the wells of salvation.*
[4] *And you will say in that day: Give thanks to the Lord,*
   call on his name;

make known his deeds among the nations;
  proclaim that his name is exalted.

[5] *Sing praises to the Lord, for he has done gloriously;*
  let this be known in all the earth.
[6] *Shout aloud and sing for joy, O royal Zion,*
  for great in your midst is the Holy One of Israel.

The opening chapters of Isaiah's prophecy offer hope to Israel in the midst of difficult times. The prophecy concerning "Immanuel" (Isa 7), the son of David who is called "Wonderful Counselor, Mighty God, Everlasting Father, and Prince of Peace" (Isa 9), and "the shoot" that will come from the stock of Jesse who will bring an age of universal peace (Isa 11)—all of these prophecies proclaim a future time of salvation for God's people on "that day" (verse 1). This chapter takes the form of a psalm of thanksgiving, a song anticipating the realization of those blessings promised in the preceding chapters.

The theme of this song is gratitude for God's salvation. The psalmist sings: "God is my salvation" (verse 2). The hymn expresses thanks for the wondrous things that God will do when he brings salvation to those who hope in him. It has many parallels to the song of Moses, a song of thanksgiving for Israel's deliverance from Egypt: "The Lord is my strength and my might, and he has become my salvation" (Exod 15:2; verse 2). Israel knows that God's anger is abated and that God has come to comfort them (verse 1). Israel is able to sing, "I will trust, and will not be afraid" (verse 2).

Throughout the Scriptures, water is frequently an expression of God's grace and blessings. The prophets used water symbolism as they looked to the future for a time of forgiveness and salvation. Isaiah anticipates the day when God's people will joyfully "draw water from the wells of salvation" (verse 3). Expressing hope for the blessings of God's spirit, the prophet proclaimed, "I will pour water on the thirsty land, and streams on the dry ground; I will pour my spirit upon your descendants, and my blessings on your offspring" (Isa 44:3). This same prophet invited all who long for life to come to its source: "Ho, everyone who thirsts, come to the waters" (Isa 55:1). God's word through his prophet Jeremiah proclaims that the Lord himself is the source of the waters of life: "They have forsaken me, the fountain of living water" (Jer 2:13).

The revelation of the Old Testament prophets is the source of Jesus' words in which he proclaims himself to be the source of life-giving water. Speaking to the woman at the well in Samaria, Jesus said to her, "Everyone who drinks of this water will be thirsty again, but those who drink of the water that I will give them will never be thirsty. The water that I will give will become in them a spring of water gushing up to eternal life" (John 4:13–14). Jesus himself is "the well of salvation" (verse 3), the font of true life, the source of God's spirit. When we drink from the water that he gives, we drink to our eternal life.

Reflection and discussion

• Why would water be such a powerful symbol for the prophets of Israel to express the blessings of God?

• How do I draw water from the well of salvation in my own Christian life today?

Prayer

Holy One, you are my strength and my salvation. I come to you thirsting for the water that will quench my thirst forever. Calm the fears of my life and help me trust in you. Give me your blessings and pour out your Spirit upon me.

On the banks, on both sides of the river, there will grow all kinds of trees for food. Their leaves will not wither nor their fruit fail, but they will bear fresh fruit every month, because the water for them flows from the sanctuary.

Ezek 47:12

Water Flowing from God's Temple

EZEKIEL 47:1–12 [1] *Then he brought me back to the entrance of the temple; there, water was flowing from below the threshold of the temple toward the east (for the temple faced east); and the water was flowing down from below the south end of the threshold of the temple, south of the altar.* [2] *Then he brought me out by way of the north gate, and led me around on the outside to the outer gate that faces toward the east; and the water was coming out on the south side.*

[3] *Going on eastward with a cord in his hand, the man measured one thousand cubits, and then led me through the water; and it was ankle-deep.* [4] *Again he measured one thousand, and led me through the water; and it was knee-deep. Again he measured one thousand, and led me through the water; and it was up to the waist.* [5] *Again he measured one thousand, and it was a river that I could not cross, for the water had risen; it was deep enough to swim in, a river that could not be crossed.* [6] *He said to me, "Mortal, have you seen this?"*

Then he led me back along the bank of the river. [7] *As I came back, I saw on the bank of the river a great many trees on the one side and on the other.* [8] *He said to*

42

me, "This water flows toward the eastern region and goes down into the Arabah; and when it enters the sea, the sea of stagnant waters, the water will become fresh. ⁹Wherever the river goes, every living creature that swarms will live, and there will be very many fish, once these waters reach there. It will become fresh; and everything will live where the river goes. ¹⁰People will stand fishing beside the sea from En-gedi to En-eglaim; it will be a place for the spreading of nets; its fish will be of a great many kinds, like the fish of the Great Sea. ¹¹But its swamps and marshes will not become fresh; they are to be left for salt. ¹²On the banks, on both sides of the river, there will grow all kinds of trees for food. Their leaves will not wither nor their fruit fail, but they will bear fresh fruit every month, because the water for them flows from the sanctuary. Their fruit will be for food, and their leaves for healing."

The visionary tour of the prophet Ezekiel begins in Jerusalem at the temple of God. There the prophet sees a stream of water flowing from within the temple sanctuary, out from beneath its threshold, and out of the temple precincts toward the east. The water continues to flow and rise as it pours down the valley east of Jerusalem and then southward into the desert (verses 1–2). The water continues to rise as it makes it way through the desert, becoming like a surging river (verse 5), following the natural contours of the land until it reaches the "sea of stagnant waters" (verse 8).

The vision conforms well to the topography of Judea. The temple sits high above the valley on Mount Zion. East of the temple foundations, the valley runs southeasterly into the Judean desert. The wilderness quickly descends from Jerusalem to the lowest place on the face of the earth, what is known today as the Dead Sea. The further east and south one travels from Jerusalem, the more dry and barren the landscape becomes. This wilderness area is a dramatic contrast to the lush vegetation and fishing industry of the Sea of Galilee to the north and the Mediterranean Sea to the west.

In Ezekiel's guided vision, this stream of water gushing from within the temple contains dramatic life-giving properties. Everywhere the prophet is led along this surging river the fresh water generates life. Trees that bear fresh fruit every month will grow along its banks (verses 7, 12), many species of fish will live in the newly-fresh water (verse 9), and fishing will prosper in the sea (verse 10). In the future day of the vision's fulfillment, what was a lifeless wilderness will become a place of fruitful abundance.

This clearly symbolic vision of God's future blessing demonstrates that God's presence in the temple brings life to a world threatened with sterility and desolation. Christian writers developed this text into a rich theology of Jesus, source of living water and of God's life-giving Spirit. In John's gospel, Jesus himself is the new temple (John 2:19) and the source of living water. He is the place where the divine presence dwells on earth, so streams of water flow from within him to give life to the world. At his death, life-giving water flowed, along with redeeming blood, as his side was pierced with a lance (John 19:34).

The final vision of John in the book of Revelation shows that Jesus himself, as God's sacrificial Lamb, is the source of the life-empowered water that flows through the New Jerusalem. John's vision of the future tells of this water which irrigates the tree of life for all people, providing fruit for nourishment and leaves for healing: "Then the angel showed me the river of the water of life, bright as crystal, flowing from the throne of God and of the Lamb through the middle of the street of the city. On either side of the river is the tree of life with its twelve kinds of fruit, producing its fruit each month; and the leaves of the tree are for the healing of the nations" (Rev 22:1–2).

Early Christian art indicates that these images from the Old and New Testaments were richly alive within the community of faith. In the catacombs, for example, there are numerous images of Moses striking the rock, signifying the water that comes from within the crucified Christ. Early mosaics depict the slain Lamb from whom a river of life flows, a symbol of the sacrificed Christ as the source of life for the world. A fifth-century inscription on a column in the church of St. John Lateran reads, "This is the fountain of life which takes its rise from the wound of Christ and washes over the whole earth."

Reflection and discussion

• What is the source of the streaming water in Ezekiel's vision? What are the effects of the water on the promised land?

• In what way do New Testament writers apply the vision of Ezekiel to Christ?

• How does early Christian art signify that the pierced heart of Christ is the source of life-giving water?

• Why is visual art sometimes more expressive than written words for communicating God's revelation?

Prayer

Lord Jesus Christ, you are the new Temple of God's presence, the slain Lamb who offers life to the world, and the wounded Savior from whose side flows the means of salvation for the world. Bring me to the fountain of life and revive me with the life-giving water of your Holy Spirit.

The sacrifice acceptable to God is a broken spirit; a broken and contrite heart, O God, you will not despise. Ps 51:17

Create in Me a Clean Heart, O God

PSALM 51:1–19

[1] *Have mercy on me, O God,*
   according to your steadfast love;
according to your abundant mercy
   blot out my transgressions.
[2] *Wash me thoroughly from my iniquity,*
   and cleanse me from my sin.

[3] *For I know my transgressions,*
   and my sin is ever before me.
[4] *Against you, you alone, have I sinned,*
   and done what is evil in your sight,
so that you are justified in your sentence
   and blameless when you pass judgment.
[5] *Indeed, I was born guilty,*
   a sinner when my mother conceived me.

⁶*You desire truth in the inward being;*
   therefore teach me wisdom in my secret heart.
⁷*Purge me with hyssop, and I shall be clean;*
   wash me, and I shall be whiter than snow.
⁸*Let me hear joy and gladness;*
   let the bones that you have crushed rejoice.
⁹*Hide your face from my sins,*
   and blot out all my iniquities.

¹⁰*Create in me a clean heart, O God,*
   and put a new and right spirit within me.
¹¹*Do not cast me away from your presence,*
   and do not take your holy spirit from me.
¹²*Restore to me the joy of your salvation,*
   and sustain in me a willing spirit.

¹³*Then I will teach transgressors your ways,*
   and sinners will return to you.
¹⁴*Deliver me from bloodshed, O God,*
   O God of my salvation,
   and my tongue will sing aloud of your deliverance.

¹⁵*O Lord, open my lips,*
   and my mouth will declare your praise.
¹⁶*For you have no delight in sacrifice;*
   if I were to give a burnt offering, you would not be pleased.
¹⁷*The sacrifice acceptable to God is a broken spirit;*
   a broken and contrite heart, O God, you will not despise.

¹⁸*Do good to Zion in your good pleasure;*
   rebuild the walls of Jerusalem,
¹⁹*then you will delight in right sacrifices,*
   in burnt offerings and whole burnt offerings;
   then bulls will be offered on your altar.

The Miserere, as this penitential psalm is popularly called, is highly personal poetry, reflecting a deep intimacy with God. The penitent pleas for God's steadfast love and abundant mercy (verse 1), while also admitting his sin (verse 3). The psalmist's awareness of sin and desire to repent is prompted by his inner conscience. He realizes that God desires truth and wisdom in his inner being, his "secret heart" (verse 6). God desires not just external change, but a deep inner transformation.

The psalmist's request, "Create in me a clean heart, O God" (verse 10), is a request for an interior change. The verb "create" in the Bible is an action of God, the act of bringing something into existence that was not there before (Gen 1:1). Because the heart is the interior center of the person, the penitent is asking God for a renewed and purified inner self.

The "spirit" designates the total person under the influence of God. The "heart" and the "spirit" together characterize the condition and direction of a person's life. A "clean heart" and a "new and right spirit" together designate a mind and will open to God, ready to praise God, trusting his lead, and true to the covenant formed in steadfast love. The language of the psalm responds to the promise of "a new heart" and "a new spirit" in the prophecy of Ezekiel (36:26) and the interior renewal announced by Jeremiah (31:33) in the new covenant.

The psalm does not reject the sacrificial system of Israel with its burnt offerings on the altar of the temple (verses 16, 19). But it states that what God desires most is a repentant heart and spirit. A "broken and contrite heart" (verse 17) is the sacrifice God wants most, and this renewed heart, turned toward God, is the prerequisite for sacrifices acceptable to God on the altar. Ritual worship of God is true adoration when it is offered by a people in whom God has created a new heart. The broken and contrite heart says to God, "I am yours, not my own."

Reflection and discussion

• Why is a clean heart something that only God can create in me? What does God do when people truly repent?

• How does genuine forgiveness create a renewed heart within us?

• What kind of sacrifice does God desire from his people? What does this tell me about my worship of God?

• Why is a transformed heart a requirement for one's worship of God to be effective (verse 17; Matthew 5:23–24)?

Prayer

Have mercy on me, O God, for your love is steadfast and your compassion is abundant. Create in me a clean and contrite heart so that my whole life will give you praise. Help me to experience the joy of forgiveness and send your Holy Spirit to live within me.

With my whole heart I seek you; do not let me stray from your commandments. I treasure your word in my heart, so that I may not sin against you.

Ps 119:10–11

Treasuring God's Word in the Heart

PSALM 119:1–16

¹*Happy are those whose way is blameless,*
who walk in the law of the Lord.
²*Happy are those who keep his decrees,*
who seek him with their whole heart,
³*who also do no wrong,*
but walk in his ways.
⁴*You have commanded your precepts*
to be kept diligently.
⁵*O that my ways may be steadfast*
in keeping your statutes!
⁶*Then I shall not be put to shame,*
having my eyes fixed on all your commandments.
⁷*I will praise you with an upright heart,*
when I learn your righteous ordinances.

⁸*I will observe your statutes;*
  do not utterly forsake me.
⁹*How can young people keep their way pure?*
  By guarding it according to your word.
¹⁰*With my whole heart I seek you;*
  do not let me stray from your commandments.
¹¹*I treasure your word in my heart,*
  so that I may not sin against you.
¹²*Blessed are you, O Lord;*
  teach me your statutes.
¹³*With my lips I declare*
  all the ordinances of your mouth.
¹⁴*I delight in the way of your decrees*
  as much as in all riches.
¹⁵*I will meditate on your precepts,*
  and fix my eyes on your ways.
¹⁶*I will delight in your statutes;*
  I will not forget your word.

This psalm is an extended meditation on what it means to "walk in the law of the Lord" (verse 1). The Hebrew word translated here as "law" is Torah. It is probably better translated as "teaching" or "instruction." The Torah never has the legalistic sense that we associate today with the word "law." The psalm, the longest by far of all the psalms, goes on for 176 verses, reflecting on what it means to live God's Torah. The frequent use of the word "way" or "ways," as a synonym for Torah, describes living Torah as a pilgrimage or life-journey. Living Torah embraces all the movements of human life with God.

The psalmist expands the reader's understanding of God's Torah in multiple ways. Torah is a way of life, learned from the writings contained in the first five books of the Bible, but not restricted to them. It is experiencing God in the present moment where the traditions of the past take on new life. Torah is personal dedication to what one understands to be God's will, but not conformity to a legal code. And, most important, it is seeking God with one's whole heart.

Life is happy and blessed for those who live God's Torah, "who seek him with their whole heart" (verse 2). This seeking God with the heart means wholehearted devotion to God's way and interiorizing God's will. The psalmist writes with the vocabulary of Deuteronomy. The central impulse of the psalm, the heart of the Torah itself, is the great commandment of Deuteronomy 6: "Love the Lord your God with all your heart" by keeping and teaching his words.

Those who live God's Torah know that God has revealed his will in many different ways, from the text of the Torah scrolls to the interior whispers of the heart. But they also know that the word of God can never be possessed; it must be continually sought. It must be studied in prayer and meditated upon so that God will give the gift of understanding. The one who walks in the law of the Lord is the one who says to God, "With my whole heart I seek you" (verse 10).

The New Testament model for this kind of wholehearted seeking God's Torah is that great daughter of Israel, Mary of Nazareth. She studied and meditated on God's word in prayer. As she prayed this psalm, "I treasure your word in my heart" (verse 11), she made its words her own. Luke's gospel says of her: "Mary treasured all these words and pondered them in her heart" (Luke 2:19). With her example, we can learn to seek God with our whole heart.

Reflection and discussion

• In what ways is Israel's understanding of Torah different from our modern understanding of law?

• What is the difference between a halfhearted and wholehearted devotion to God's way?

• In what way is Mary of Nazareth a model for walking in the way of God's Torah?

• What does it mean for me to treasure God's word in my heart? What are the implications for my study of Scripture?

Prayer

Lord of the Torah, you reveal your ways to your people and teach them your will. Help me to seek you with my whole heart and to delight in the way of your commands. Give me the joy of studying your word as I treasure your word in my heart.

Set me as a seal upon your heart; for love is strong as death, passion fierce as the grave. Its flashes are flashes of fire, a raging flame. Song 8:6

Bride of My Heart

SONG OF SONGS 4:9–10

[9]*You have ravished my heart, my sister, my bride,*
you have ravished my heart with a glance of your eyes,
with one jewel of your necklace.
[10]*How sweet is your love, my sister, my bride!*
how much better is your love than wine,
and the fragrance of your oils than any spice!

SONG OF SONGS 8:6–7

[6]*Set me as a seal upon your heart,*
as a seal upon your arm;
for love is strong as death,
passion fierce as the grave.
Its flashes are flashes of fire,
a raging flame.
[7]*Many waters cannot quench love,*
neither can floods drown it.

If one offered for love
all the wealth of his house,
it would be utterly scorned.

The Song of Songs is a collection of love poetry. The two lovers are single-minded in their devotion to each other and to their relationship. When together, they speak of delight in each other's presence; when apart, they express desire for the absent lover. Though they must often part, they issue repeated invitations to one another. The imagery seems to express the natural harmony between men and women and between humanity and the natural world which was characteristic of God's original creation.

In the first selection, the man speaks, addressing the woman with a series of admiring exclamations (4:9–10). "Sister" and "bride" are terms of endearment, not of kinship or marriage. "You have ravished my heart" means that she has completely captivated him. A mere glance of her eye or one jewel of her necklace completely enchants him. Her love gives much more pleasure than the enjoyable bouquet and intoxicating qualities of wine, and the oils she uses to anoint herself surpass the scents of even the most exotic spices. He is completely enthralled by her.

The woman speaks in the second selection, stating her longing to be intimately joined to the man she loves (8:6–7). "Set me like a seal upon your heart" conveys her desire to be always with him. Seals were symbols of personal identity, representing the owner's influence and honor. She wants the relationship to be as inseparable, intimate, and distinctive as is the link between the man and his personal seal.

The following images all describe some dimension of genuine love. It is as tenacious and irresistible as death and the grave. Love's intensity is such that its sparks of fire become an uncontainable, raging flame. Even the sea and raging floods cannot overwhelm or extinguish it. True love, finally, is priceless. Even if one were to risk house and possessions to acquire it, it is futile to try to buy love. If genuine love cannot be overwhelmed by the cosmic forces of death, fire, and flood, then surely no material wealth can be considered a means to acquire love.

The biblical writer realized that the love between a man and woman does not exhaust the power of love as God's supreme gift to his creation. The Song of Songs invites readers to explore the celebration of love on every level of existence. Both Jewish and Christian commentators through the ages have taken an allegorical approach and interpreted the text as a celebration of the divine/human relationship. The imagery of the poetry reflects aspects of covenantal love and the heart serves as a tangible metaphor for the intimacy of divine and human love.

Reflection and discussion

• Complete this sentence: "Love is…." Why is the heart an ideal metaphor for love?

• Is human love poetry appropriate for expressing the love between God and his people? In what way is sexual love a fitting image for the love of God?

Prayer

Eternal and merciful God, your compassionate and committed love is the foundation of your covenant. Let me experience the passion of your love for me and the fact that I am precious and beloved in your eyes. May I respond by loving you with all my heart.

SUGGESTIONS FOR FACILITATORS, GROUP SESSION 3

1. Welcome group members and ask if there are any announcements anyone would like to make.

2. You may want to pray this prayer as a group:

Holy God of Israel, we praise you for the ways you constantly refresh and revive your people with the waters of life. You gave them water from the rock in the wilderness, offer them water from the wells of salvation, and promise them water from the temple to renew the whole earth. Quench the thirsts of our longings hearts, teach us to seek you with all our hearts, and create clean and contrite hearts within us. As we study your ancient Scriptures, help us encourage one another with hope and guide us with your Spirit of truth.

3. Ask one or more of the following questions:
   - Which image from the lessons this week stands out most memorably to you?
   - What is the most important lesson you learned through your study this week?

4. Discuss lessons 7 through 12. Choose one or more of the questions for reflection and discussion from each lesson to discuss as a group. You may want to ask group members which question was most challenging or helpful to them as you review each lesson.

5. Remember that there are no definitive answers for these discussion questions. The insights of group members will add to the understanding of all. None of these questions require an expert.

6. After talking about each lesson, instruct group members to complete lessons 13 through 18 on their own during the six days before the next group meeting. They should write out their own answers to the questions as preparation for next week's group discussion.

7. Ask the group if anyone is having any particular problems with the Bible study during the week. You may want to share advice and encouragement within the group.

8. Conclude by praying aloud together the prayer at the end of one of the lessons discussed. You may add to the prayer based on the sharing that has occurred in the group.

No one has ever seen God. It is God the only Son, who is close to the Father's heart, who has made him known. John 1:18

Close to the Father's Heart

JOHN 1:1–5, 14, 16–18 *¹In the beginning was the Word, and the Word was with God, and the Word was God. ²He was in the beginning with God. ³All things came into being through him, and without him not one thing came into being. What has come into being ⁴in him was life, and the life was the light of all people. ⁵The light shines in the darkness, and the darkness did not overcome it.*

¹⁴And the Word became flesh and lived among us, and we have seen his glory, the glory as of a father's only son, full of grace and truth. ¹⁶From his fullness we have all received, grace upon grace. ¹⁷The law indeed was given through Moses; grace and truth came through Jesus Christ. ¹⁸No one has ever seen God. It is God the only Son, who is close to the Father's heart, who has made him known.

The writer of the fourth gospel has been called the evangelist of the heart of Jesus. In passages from the gospel of John, the heart of Jesus is shown to be the fountain of living water from which those who believe in him draw grace and truth. But the gospel also demonstrates that God the Father is the ultimate source of all that fills the heart of Jesus. Jesus is able to reveal and share the life of God with humanity because of his intimate, heart-to-heart unity with the Father. The unseen God is made known to the world through his Son: "It is God the only Son, who is close to the Father's heart, who has made him known" (verse 18).

A human word is, in a sense, the extension of a person to others; the divine Word is God's reaching out, seeking to share his divine being, sharing eternal love with creation. A human word reveals hidden thoughts; the divine Word reveals the hidden nature of God, demonstrating that God is loving, caring, and forgiving. As the Father's full and perfect expression of himself, Jesus is "the Word" (verse 1). All that God is, the Word also is. Before time began, this Word was with God, constantly oriented toward God, perfectly one with God, yet at the same time distinct from God. The first words of John's gospel, "in the beginning," also the first words of the Old Testament, indicate that there will be a new beginning in the coming of God's word into the world. In the coming of God's Son to the world, humanity will be created anew, and God will communicate his own life to those who receive his Son.

God's word was partially manifested through creation, then through the Torah, and finally and fully, through Jesus Christ, the Word made flesh (verse 14). The deeds and words of Jesus are the deeds and words of God. Though "no one has ever seen God" (verse 18), we have seen the glory of the Son (verse 14), shining out in the world's darkness. The Son is the manifestation of God in a way that we can understand, a way that is both fully divine and fully human.

The purpose of the Son's coming into the world is so that we might share intimately in God's life. Because Jesus is "full of grace and truth," we have all received from his fullness, "grace upon grace" (verse 16). Jesus, "who is close to the Father's heart" (verse 18) has made God known to us. From his eternal existence with the Father, throughout his historical existence on earth, and now with the Father in risen glory, the Son is always close to the Father's heart. The love of the Father for the Son and the love of the Son for the Father overflow into our humanity. Though the Greek word translated here as "heart" can also be translated as bosom, breast, or chest, the sense of the word is that Jesus is always united with the Father in the most intimate way. Jesus experiences the intimate love of the Father as closely as possible. The image is that of a child at the mother's breast or a lover resting near the beating heart of the beloved. As the gospel of John tells us throughout, this is the intimate love of God that Jesus wants us to share through him.

Reflection and discussion

• What are the ways that I experience the self-revelation of God in the world?

• What does it mean for my life that the divine Word became flesh in the world?

• When have I felt most close to God? In what way was it like resting close to God's heart (verse 18)?

Prayer

Word made Flesh, you are eternally close to the heart of your Father and you communicate God's love to humanity. Teach me how to receive from the fullness of your grace and truth so that I may experience the intimacy of God's love.

Let anyone who is thirsty come to me, and let the one who believes in me drink. As the scripture has said, "Out of the believer's heart shall flow rivers of living water." John 7:37–38

Source of Living Water

JOHN 4:7–15 ⁷*A Samaritan woman came to draw water, and Jesus said to her, "Give me a drink."* ⁸*(His disciples had gone to the city to buy food.)* ⁹*The Samaritan woman said to him, "How is it that you, a Jew, ask a drink of me, a woman of Samaria?" (Jews do not share things in common with Samaritans.)* ¹⁰*Jesus answered her, "If you knew the gift of God, and who it is that is saying to you, 'Give me a drink,' you would have asked him, and he would have given you living water."* ¹¹*The woman said to him, "Sir, you have no bucket, and the well is deep. Where do you get that living water?* ¹²*Are you greater than our ancestor Jacob, who gave us the well, and with his sons and his flocks drank from it?"* ¹³*Jesus said to her, "Everyone who drinks of this water will be thirsty again,* ¹⁴*but those who drink of the water that I will give them will never be thirsty. The water that I will give will become in them a spring of water gushing up to eternal life."* ¹⁵*The woman said to him, "Sir, give me this water, so that I may never be thirsty or have to keep coming here to draw water."*

JOHN 7:37–39 ³⁷*On the last day of the festival, the great day, while Jesus was standing there, he cried out, "Let anyone who is thirsty come to me,* ³⁸*and let* *the one who believes in me drink. As the scripture has said, 'Out of the believer's heart shall flow rivers of living water.'* [39] *Now he said this about the Spirit, which believers in him were to receive; for as yet there was no Spirit, because Jesus was not yet glorified.*

Within the human heart there is a thirst that only a sharing in God's life can satisfy. The psalmist expressed this longing: "My soul thirsts for God, for the living God" (Ps 42:2). It is the yearning of which St. Augustine prayed: "You have made us for yourself, O God, and our hearts are restless until they find rest in you." In the Scriptures, God responds to this longing of the heart, and that response is often expressed through images of water. The psalmist sang of God, "With you is the fountain of life" (Ps 36:9). Jeremiah called God "the fountain of living water" (Jer 17:13). In God's promised future "a fountain shall be opened for the house of David and the inhabitants of Jerusalem" (Zech 13:1), and "living waters shall flow out from Jerusalem" (Zech 14:8).

When John's gospel proclaims Jesus as the source of living water, it is expressing the truth that Jesus is what humanity has been longing for. To the woman at the well in Samaria, Jesus contrasted the water of Jacob's well to the "living water" that he will give (4:10–14). The water Jesus gives quenches the heart's thirst for God. It will become within those who drink it "a spring of water gushing up to eternal life." This water not only quenches thirst, but it is an eternal self-replenishing spring. It offers a new kind of life, an abundant and everlasting life in God's Spirit.

On the last day of the feast of Tabernacles (also called the feast of Booths) Jesus invited everyone to quench their thirst in him: "Let anyone who is thirsty come to me, and let the one who believes in me drink" (7:37–38). As the priest poured out the water upon the temple's altar of sacrifice, commemorating the water that gushed from the rock during the exodus (Exod 17:6), Jesus proclaimed that Israel's yearnings for everlasting waters will be satisfied.

As evidence for Israel's hope, Jesus quoted Scripture: "Out of his heart shall flow rivers of living water" (7:38). There are two questions concerning this verse: whose heart is referred to, and what is its biblical source? The verse could mean that the living waters flow from the heart of Jesus, or as this translation assumes, from the heart of the one who believes in Jesus. The context suggests that the verse refers to the heart of Jesus, since the thirsty believer goes to Jesus for refreshment. But in either translation, the source of the flowing water is Jesus himself.

The other question about this Scripture verse concerns its biblical source. The closest Old Testament references to this text concern the water flowing from the rock in the wilderness (Exod 17:6) and the river of water flowing from the temple (Ezek 47:1–12). The psalmist referred to the rock in the wilderness: "He made streams come out of the rock, and caused waters to flow down like rivers" (Ps 78:16). Zechariah referred to the water from the temple: "Living waters shall flow out from Jerusalem" (Zech 14:8). The early Christians saw the fulfillment of these texts in Jesus, who is both the living rock and the new temple from which the waters flow. Justin Martyr, in the second century, identified Jesus as the Rock and Christians as those who were "quarried from the heart of Christ."

Jesus' promise, "Out of his heart shall flow rivers of living water" (7:38), points to a future time because Jesus has not yet been glorified (verse 39). The perfection of this promise is linked, in John's gospel, with the crucifixion and death of Jesus. At the cross the Spirit will be given and the fountain of redeeming grace will flow from Christ's heart to renew the world.

Reflection and discussion

• What is the deepest thirst of my heart? What verse or image of the Bible eases my thirst?

• Why is the teaching of Jesus so effective with the Samaritan woman? How does Jesus move from natural thirst to a promise of his abundant life?

• Why did Jesus proclaim himself as the source of living water on the Jewish feast that memorialized the Israelite journey through the wilderness?

• In what ways do the living rock and the temple from which water flows foreshadow the sacred heart of Jesus?

• How have I experienced the abundance of the Holy Spirit flowing through me?

Prayer

Font of Living Water, you quench my deepest thirsts. Open my heart to you so that the waters of life may flow through me, cleansing, refreshing, and giving me abundant and eternal life.

One of his disciples—the one whom Jesus loved—was reclining next to him.
John 13:23

Close to the Heart of Jesus

JOHN 13:1–5, 20–30 ¹*Now before the festival of the Passover, Jesus knew that his hour had come to depart from this world and go to the Father. Having loved his own who were in the world, he loved them to the end.* ²*The devil had already put it into the heart of Judas son of Simon Iscariot to betray him. And during supper* ³*Jesus, knowing that the Father had given all things into his hands, and that he had come from God and was going to God,* ⁴*got up from the table, took off his outer robe, and tied a towel around himself.* ⁵*Then he poured water into a basin and began to wash the disciples' feet and to wipe them with the towel that was tied around him.*

²⁰*"Very truly, I tell you, whoever receives one whom I send receives me; and whoever receives me receives him who sent me."* ²¹*After saying this Jesus was troubled in spirit, and declared, "Very truly, I tell you, one of you will betray me."* ²²*The disciples looked at one another, uncertain of whom he was speaking.* ²³*One of his disciples—the one whom Jesus loved—was reclining next to him;* ²⁴*Simon Peter therefore motioned to him to ask Jesus of whom he was speaking.* ²⁵*So while reclining next to Jesus, he asked him, "Lord, who is it?"* ²⁶*Jesus answered, "It is the one to whom I give this piece of bread when I have dipped it in the dish." So when he had dipped the piece of bread, he gave it to Judas son of Simon Iscariot.* ²⁷*After*

he received the piece of bread, Satan entered into him. Jesus said to him, "Do quickly what you are going to do." ²⁸Now no one at the table knew why he said this to him. ²⁹Some thought that, because Judas had the common purse, Jesus was telling him, "Buy what we need for the festival"; or, that he should give something to the poor. ³⁰So, after receiving the piece of bread, he immediately went out. And it was night.

When the time had come for the departure of Jesus from this world, he knew that his passage would be the supreme demonstration of his love for his disciples. Despite their ignorance, denial, and betrayal, Jesus knew they were "his own," and he loved them in their failures (verse 1). In order to express the completeness of his love, we are told that Jesus loved his own "to the end." This expression of love has two meanings: Jesus loved them to the end of his life, and he loved them in the fullest possible sense. The remainder of the passion account, from the washing of his disciples' feet to his climactic death on the cross, is a consummate act of love. Knowing that both his origin and his destiny were in the Father, from whom he had come and to whom he was returning (verse 3), Jesus began his final and ultimate gift of self.

In his final hours, Jesus not only revealed his own unconditional love for his disciples, but he revealed the love of God for the world. Despite the continual failure of his disciples and even his ultimate betrayal, Jesus demonstrated the love of God that surpasses all imagining through his total gift. As the spotlight turns to Judas, the betrayer of Jesus (verse 21), Jesus dipped a piece of bread in a dish and handed it to this most despised character in the gospel (verse 26). In displaying never-failing love, a love that reached out even to this failed and disloyal disciple, Jesus displayed the unsurpassed love of God, a love to the end. Yet despite love offered, Judas walked out into the darkness of the night (verse 30).

In stark contrast to the failure and betrayal of his disciples, John's gospel presents one of the disciples of Jesus—"the one whom Jesus loved" (verse 23). This beloved disciple was most probably an historical disciple, the witness and author of this gospel (John 21:20, 24), but he is also the gospel's model for discipleship. The character of the beloved disciple in his relationship with Jesus is the ideal held out for all who read the gospel. This model disciple is in relationship to Jesus as Jesus is in relationship to the Father.

The posture of the disciple whom Jesus loved is described three times in the gospel, twice here and once at the end of the gospel. The words describing the beloved disciple as "reclining next to Jesus," are actually the same words used at the beginning of the gospel to say that the Son is "close to the Father's heart" (1:18). The beloved disciple is, literally, "in the bosom" of Jesus (verse 23; 21:20), or "on the breast/chest" of Jesus (verse 25). The words consciously duplicate the position of the Son with the Father in order to demonstrate the closeness of a true disciple to Jesus. The ideal disciple is one who is close to the heart of Jesus.

Reflection and discussion

• What is the meaning of love "to the end" (verse 1)? What does this indicate about the quality of Jesus' love?

• How does Jesus show love "to the end" even to Judas? How could Judas refuse such love?

• In what way does John's gospel show that the relationship of Jesus and his disciples is patterned on the relationship of Jesus and his Father?

• How does the gospel contrast the disciple close to the heart of Jesus with the other disciples? How does the gospel portray this disciple as a model for all disciples?

• The gospel portrays the ideal disciple as one who is close to the heart of Jesus. What does it mean to me to be close to the heart of Jesus?

Prayer

Suffering Lord, you loved your disciples to the end. Help me to be faithful to you in difficult times and to trust in your undying love for me. Draw me ever closer to your Sacred Heart so that I may experience the divine love which you share with your Father forever.

This is my commandment, that you love one another as I have loved you.

John 15:12

No Greater Love

JOHN 13:33–35 ³³*"Little children, I am with you only a little longer. You will look for me; and as I said to the Jews so now I say to you, 'Where I am going, you cannot come.' ³⁴I give you a new commandment, that you love one another. Just as I have loved you, you also should love one another. ³⁵By this everyone will know that you are my disciples, if you have love for one another."*

JOHN 15:9–13 ⁹*"As the Father has loved me, so I have loved you; abide in my love. ¹⁰If you keep my commandments, you will abide in my love, just as I have kept my Father's commandments and abide in his love. ¹¹I have said these things to you so that my joy may be in you, and that your joy may be complete. ¹²This is my commandment, that you love one another as I have loved you. ¹³No one has greater love than this, to lay down one's life for one's friends."*

Since Jesus had come from the Father and was returning to the Father, he would no longer be physically present with his disciples (13:33). Yet they can continue to be his disciples and keep his Spirit alive among themselves as they continue their life in the world. The world will still encounter Jesus and he will continue to be present among his disciples as they follow his "new commandment" and love as he loved (13:34).

The commandment that Jesus gave his disciples—"Just as I have loved you, you also should love one another"—is at once very old and totally new. It is based on God's ancient commandment, "You shall love your neighbor as yourself" (Lev 19:18). It is new because it is the commandment of the new covenant, the new relationship between God and his people founded on the self-giving life and sacrificial death of Jesus. It is new because the love itself is new; it is the love of Jesus being shared in a communion of love by his disciples. The full sense of the commandment would be better expressed: "With the love with which I have loved you, love one another." Jesus is not just a person from the past whom his disciples are called to imitate. Rather, his disciples love with his love. Jesus himself and his self-giving love become present in the mutual love of his disciples.

This love of Jesus within his followers is to be a clear and unmistakable sign of Christian discipleship: "By this everyone will know that you are my disciples" (13:35). Christians recognize one another by a single sign—loving with the love of Christ. The community of disciples, Christ's church, continues to be a witness for the world, just as Jesus was a manifestation of divine love within the world. If this love is lacking, the presence of Christ in our world through his church can no longer be seen. When we fail to love, we discredit Christ's church and we hide Christ's presence from the eyes of others. By demonstrating the love of Christ, we become an effective sign that overcomes the unbelief of the world.

This love of the Son, eternally "close to the Father's heart" (1:18), is ultimately a gift from the Father, creating a chain of relationships between the Father, Son, and disciples. Jesus said to his disciples, "As the Father has loved me, so I have loved you" (15:9). The Father's love for his Son is the source of Jesus' love for his disciples, so that the whole act of love shown by Jesus to his disciples is the communication of God's gift of love through his Son. The result of this love is a deep and full joy that Jesus wants his disciples to experience (15:11). For Jesus this joy consists in being loved by the Father and in responding out of love to him. Disciples experience a share in the joy of Jesus as they participate in Jesus' loving oneness with the Father.

The eternal love of the Father for the Son was lived out by Jesus in his earthly life and reached its climax on the cross. The crucified Jesus is the way the Father's love is most manifested in the world, and it is the way to the Father for the disciples of Jesus. With the self-giving love demonstrated by

Jesus on the cross, disciples are to manifest their love for one another: "No one has greater love than this, to lay down one's life for one's friends" (15:13). The measure of the disciples' love for one another is the supreme act of Jesus' love for them, his love "to the end" (13:1).

Reflection and discussion

• Why has the word "love" lost much of its convincing power today?

• In what way is the commandment of Jesus "new" (13:34; 15:12)? Why does the new covenant need a new commandment?

• If my love for others is the only real witness to Christ and the unmistakable sign of discipleship, what happens when I fail to love?

• What gives me the greatest and most lasting joy? In what way is this joy a result of the Father's love?

• The Russian novelist, Fyodor Dostoevsky, wrote, "Love in action is a harsh and dreadful thing compared with love in dreams." In what way does Christian love demonstrate this truth?

• When I look back on my life at its end, what are the things that will determine the quality of my life?

Prayer

Loving Savior, you love your disciples with the love you have received from your Father. With this love from the Father's heart, you create a community of disciples manifesting that love for the world. Help me to be a witness to your love so that the world may come to believe in you.

One of the soldiers pierced his side with a spear, and at once blood and water came out. John 19:34

The Pierced Side of Jesus

JOHN 19:31–37 ³¹*Since it was the day of Preparation, the Jews did not want the bodies left on the cross during the sabbath, especially because that sabbath was a day of great solemnity. So they asked Pilate to have the legs of the crucified men broken and the bodies removed.* ³²*Then the soldiers came and broke the legs of the first and of the other who had been crucified with him.* ³³*But when they came to Jesus and saw that he was already dead, they did not break his legs.* ³⁴*Instead, one of the soldiers pierced his side with a spear, and at once blood and water came out.* ³⁵*(He who saw this has testified so that you also may believe. His testimony is true, and he knows that he tells the truth.)* ³⁶*These things occurred so that the scripture might be fulfilled, "None of his bones shall be broken."* ³⁷*And again another passage of scripture says, "They will look on the one whom they have pierced."*

The bodies of the crucified had to be removed from their place of torture by sundown, the beginning of Passover. After breaking the legs of those crucified with Jesus to hasten their death, the soldiers came to Jesus and saw that he seemed to be already dead (verses 32–33). In order to confirm his death, a soldier thrust his lance into the chest of Jesus, intending to reach the most vital organ, his heart. Roman soldiers were trained to plunge toward the heart in battle against an enemy, or in offering the decisive thrust of mercy—the *coup de grace*—the finishing stroke delivered to one mortally wounded. As the side of Jesus was pierced, the narrator carefully notes, "blood and water came out" (verse 34).

Yet, as is characteristic of John's gospel, historical specifics are rarely mentioned without referring to a deeper level of significance. The author's treatment of the flow of blood and water from Jesus' crucified body points toward a fuller meaning than an incidental detail. This wondrous occurrence is backed by the testimony of a witness, and the author insists on the truthfulness of his testimony (verse 35). The evangelist, passing on this account to a new generation several decades after Christ's death, wanted his readers to have no doubt that blood and water flowed from within Jesus for the sake of their belief.

The blood expresses the sacrificial death of Jesus, offered for the world's redemption. Jewish law, as codified in the Mishnah, insisted that when the priest offered animal sacrifice at the temple, he should slit the heart of the sacrificial victim and make the blood come forth. The thrust of the lance into the heart of Jesus indicates that he is the Lamb of God, the paschal victim sacrificed for the world's salvation. The notation that "none of his bones shall be broken" (verse 36), an Old Testament quotation referring to the lamb to be offered on Passover (Exod 12:46; Num 9:12), further points to the sacrificial and redemptive nature of Jesus' death.

The water expresses the new life communicated to the world through Christ's ultimate expression of love. Out of the pierced heart of the Crucified One flows rivers of living water (7:38). From within Christ's body comes that "spring of water gushing up to eternal life" (4:14). Those who drink from the water flowing from his side discover the waters that will quench their thirst forever. Here is the true Rock from which the water flows, giving drink to God's thirsty people on their journey (Num 20:11; 1 Cor 10:4). Here is the water flowing from the new Temple, bringing healing and fruitfulness to the wilderness (Ezek 47:1–12).

The final Scripture quoted is from Zechariah 12:10, "They will look on the one whom they have pierced" (verse 37). Zechariah was speaking about the mourning and weeping of Jerusalem over the death of a first-born son. In John's gospel those who look on the Pierced One are those who witnessed the crucifixion and those believers of later generations who come to understand the significance of his saving death. The life of Jesus continues to flow into his church, offering to the Jews and Gentiles of the new covenant the quenching water of the Holy Spirit and the redeeming blood of Christ's sacrifice. As his church continues to look on the wounded though glorified body of Jesus, God's people receive new life in the water of baptism and renew the sacrifice of Christ's blood in Eucharist. Despite the physical absence of Jesus, he is still present to his church in every generation through his Holy Spirit and through the water and blood of his sacraments.

Reflection and discussion

• In what way does John show Jesus to be the Lamb of God who takes away the sin of the world?

• Why does the gospel writer take such care to emphasize the piercing of Jesus' side and the flow of blood and water?

• In what ways does this detail of Christ's passion express the new life that flows from Christ's crucified and risen body into his church?

• How does the blood and water express God's divine mercy for humanity? How does the gospel express many layers of meaning in this single image?

• Spend some time meditating before a crucifix. What are some of my thoughts, feelings, and reflections?

Prayer

Crucified Redeemer, from your sacred heart blood and water poured out for the community of your disciples. As I gaze upon your pierced side, you offer to me the blood of the covenant and the water of new life. Thank you for your Spirit through whom you give me the grace of eternal life.

"Put your finger here and see my hands. Reach out your hand and put it in my side. Do not doubt but believe." John 20:27

The Glorious Wounds of Christ

JOHN 20:19–31 ¹⁹*When it was evening on that day, the first day of the week, and the doors of the house where the disciples had met were locked for fear of the Jews, Jesus came and stood among them and said, "Peace be with you."* ²⁰*After he said this, he showed them his hands and his side. Then the disciples rejoiced when they saw the Lord.* ²¹*Jesus said to them again, "Peace be with you. As the Father has sent me, so I send you."* ²²*When he had said this, he breathed on them and said to them, "Receive the Holy Spirit.* ²³*If you forgive the sins of any, they are forgiven them; if you retain the sins of any, they are retained."*

²⁴*But Thomas (who was called the Twin), one of the twelve, was not with them when Jesus came.* ²⁵*So the other disciples told him, "We have seen the Lord." But he said to them, "Unless I see the mark of the nails in his hands, and put my finger in the mark of the nails and my hand in his side, I will not believe."*

²⁶*A week later his disciples were again in the house, and Thomas was with them. Although the doors were shut, Jesus came and stood among them and said, "Peace be with you."* ²⁷*Then he said to Thomas, "Put your finger here and see my hands. Reach out your hand and put it in my side. Do not doubt but believe."*

[28] *Thomas answered him, "My Lord and my God!"* [29] *Jesus said to him, "Have you believed because you have seen me? Blessed are those who have not seen and yet have come to believe."*

[30] *Now Jesus did many other signs in the presence of his disciples, which are not written in this book.* [31] *But these are written so that you may come to believe that Jesus is the Messiah, the Son of God, and that through believing you may have life in his name.*

The appearance of the risen Jesus moves the disciples from a state of fear to the experience of joy and wonderment (verses 19–20). The Lord's greeting, "Peace be with you," offers them a deep confidence that dispels fear and is full of hope. Along with his gift of peace, Jesus showed the disciples the wounds in his hands and his side. They knew that the risen Jesus is the person they had seen lifted up on the cross and whose side had been pierced with the lance. This realization immediately brought joy to the disciples in the midst of their confusion and grief.

The mandate Jesus gives to his disciples is a summary of his life and ours: "As the Father has sent me, so I send you" (verse 21). Out of love for the world, God sent his Son (3:16). With the love of the Father in his heart, Jesus revealed that love to the world through his teachings, his healing signs, and through his total self-gift on the cross. Now Jesus sends his disciples on that same mission, filled with his love in their hearts. As his disciples, we are to be to the world what Jesus has been to the world. We are to embody the Father's love, to teach and heal, to comfort and bring peace, to love as Jesus loved. Jesus enlivened and empowered his disciples as he breathed on them and said, "Receive the Holy Spirit" (verse 22). As God breathed his own life into the first human beings (Gen 2:7), Jesus breathed his Spirit into God's new creation, the community of disciples sent by the risen Lord into the world.

The glorious wounds of Jesus are detailed three times in this resurrection narrative. After Jesus shows his wounds to the disciples (verse 20), Thomas, who was absent, demands to put his finger in the mark of the nails and his hand into Christ's wounded side before he will believe (verse 25). Finally, the risen Lord invites Thomas to experience his wounds and believe: "Put your finger here and see my hands. Reach out your hand and put it in my side. Do not doubt but believe" (verse 27). The invitation alone drew Thomas to answer with a great profession of faith in the divinity of Jesus: "My Lord and my God!" (verse 28).

The loving hands of Jesus reaching out to the world had been stabbed with nails; his infinitely precious heart had been pierced with a lance. The Lord of glory still bears the marks of those wounds in his eternal self-offering to the Father. Those glorious wounds tell us, far better than words could tell, that all the sufferings of humanity are echoed always in the very heart of God. Ours is a compassionate God, a God who suffers with us. Jesus, the wounded Lord, offers peace and joy to all who believe in him.

The Sacred Heart of Jesus is an eternally pierced heart. After Jesus loved his disciples to the end, God drew the heart of Jesus into divine glory, where it still beats for us and with us. From that sacred heart our Lord continues to pour out upon us the precious blood of redemption and the living waters of salvation.

Reflection and discussion

• The mission that the Father gave to Jesus is the mission that Jesus gave to his disciples. In what way does this mission define the purpose of my life on earth?

• How did the risen Lord lead Thomas to faith? In what way can doubt lead to a deeper faith?

• Why does John's gospel emphasize the wounds of Christ's passion on his resurrected body?

• How is devotion to Christ's sacred heart intimately related to the eucharistic sacrifice of his church?

• What personal meaning does the pierced and glorified heart of Jesus offer to me?

Prayer

Wounded and risen Lord, the suffering of humanity is echoed in your compassionate heart. Help me understand that no suffering is wasted in your plan for me. Make the wounds of my life a means for me to offer compassion, forgiveness, and healing to others.

SUGGESTIONS FOR FACILITATORS, GROUP SESSION 4

1. Welcome group members and ask if anyone has any questions, announcements, or requests.

2. You may want to pray this prayer as a group:

Word Made Flesh, you came into our world to reveal God's eternal love for creation. Because you are eternally close to the Father's heart, you communicate divine truth and life to the world. Through the springs of living water and the flow of redeeming blood from your sacred heart, you gave to your church the sacramental life of your eternal presence. Make us witnesses of your love and help us to love one another with the love you have given to us.

3. Ask one or more of the following questions:
   • What is the most difficult part of this study for you?
   • What insights stands out to you from the lessons this week?

4. Discuss lessons 13 through 18. Choose one or more of the questions for reflection and discussion from each lesson to discuss as a group. You may want to ask group members which question was most challenging or helpful to them as you review each lesson.

5. Keep the discussion moving, but allow time for the questions that provoke the most discussion. Encourage the group members to use "I" language in their responses.

6. After talking over each lesson, instruct group members to complete lessons 19 through 24 on their own during the six days before the next group meeting. They should write out their own answers to the questions as preparation for next week's session.

7. Ask the group what encouragement they need for the coming week. Ask the members to pray for the needs of one another during the week.

8. Conclude by praying aloud together the prayer at the end of one of the lessons discussed. You may choose to conclude the prayer by asking members to pray aloud any requests they may have.

Take my yoke upon you, and learn from me; for I am gentle and humble in heart, and you will find rest for your souls. Matt 11:29

The Humble Heart of Jesus

MATTHEW 11:25–30 *²⁵At that time Jesus said, "I thank you, Father, Lord of heaven and earth, because you have hidden these things from the wise and the intelligent and have revealed them to infants; ²⁶yes, Father, for such was your gracious will. ²⁷All things have been handed over to me by my Father; and no one knows the Son except the Father, and no one knows the Father except the Son and anyone to whom the Son chooses to reveal him.*

²⁸"Come to me, all you that are weary and are carrying heavy burdens, and I will give you rest. ²⁹Take my yoke upon you, and learn from me; for I am gentle and humble in heart, and you will find rest for your souls. ³⁰For my yoke is easy, and my burden is light."

Jesus' unique unity with God and his role as God's revealer make our response to him imperative. In John's gospel, Jesus is the revelation of the Father because he is the incarnate Word of God; here Jesus is the revelation of God because he is divine wisdom in human form. Jesus offers the great invitation "Come to me" (verse 28), like the invitation offered by personified wisdom in Proverbs 8. He is the giver of rest and comfort to those who are weary and burdened.

In the book of Sirach, "yoke" is an image of wisdom's teaching. Wisdom invites those who seek, "Draw near to me," then wisdom urges them, "Put your neck under her yoke, and let your souls receive instruction. See with your own eyes that I have labored but little and found for myself much serenity" (Sir 51:23, 26–27). Matthew's gospel presents Jesus as the Wisdom of God who invites the seeker to accept his teaching: "Take my yoke upon you, and learn from me" (verse 29). In Jesus, the teacher and the subject taught are one and the same since he embodies all that he teaches. He is divine wisdom; his teaching is a yoke that is "easy," a burden that is "light" (verse 30). Though the teaching of Jesus is demanding and challenging, it is a yoke that fits comfortably and is not burdensome for the true disciple. The yoke is light because the teaching of Jesus is focused on the essentials of justice, mercy, and love, and because it consists of personal obedience to Jesus himself.

The disciple finds the teachings of Jesus to be a gentle yoke because of the quality of his heart. The heart of Jesus is one that is "gentle and humble" (verse 29). The prophets and psalms describe these qualities as belonging to people who are poor and simple, dependent on God and trusting in him. They are the qualities that Jesus taught in the Beatitudes (Matt 5:3–12). Jesus can invite the poor, the weary, and the burdened to come to him because he is one of them. Disciples learn from him by imitating the qualities of his heart. Those who wish to cultivate within their own hearts the qualities of Jesus must focus on the simple, unspectacular, relational virtues like patience, gentleness, kindness, simplicity, humility, warmth, and cordiality.

Jesus' prayer of thanksgiving, addressed "Father, Lord of heaven and earth" (verse 25), expresses the same blend of intimacy and reverence as he expressed in the Lord's Prayer. He praises God because he has revealed divine wisdom to "infants," to the poor, humble, and trusting, rather than to "the wise and the intelligent." It has always been God's gracious will to resist the proud and give grace to the humble (verse 26). God has handed Jesus the fullness of divine wisdom (verse 27). Because Jesus alone knows the will of God fully, those who want to know the will of God must look to Jesus and follow his teachings. In order to fittingly form our hearts, we must look to the gentle and humble heart of Jesus.

Reflection and discussion

• Why is God's revelation hidden from "the wise and the intelligent" but revealed to "infants"? In what ways can I make myself more receptive to God's wisdom?

• In what way are the teachings of Jesus like a yoke upon me? Is that yoke burdensome, challenging, abrasive, easy, light, well-fitted?

• The virtues Paul recommends for Christians are similar to the qualities of the heart of Jesus (Col 3:12). How can I clothe myself with these virtues?

Prayer

Jesus, meek and humble of heart, form my heart to be like your own. Teach me wisdom so that I may know and follow the will of the Father. Give me the gentle virtues of kindness, patience, and humility so I can show the qualities of your heart to all those I meet.

"To love him with all the heart, and with all the understanding, and with all the strength," and "to love one's neighbor as oneself,"—this is much more important than all whole burnt offerings and sacrifices. Mark 12:33

Love of God and Neighbor

MARK 12:28–34 [28]*One of the scribes came near and heard them disputing with one another, and seeing that he answered them well, he asked him, "Which commandment is the first of all?"* [29]*Jesus answered, "The first is, 'Hear, O Israel: the Lord our God, the Lord is one;* [30]*you shall love the Lord your God with all your heart, and with all your soul, and with all your mind, and with all your strength.'* [31]*The second is this, 'You shall love your neighbor as yourself.' There is no other commandment greater than these."* [32]*Then the scribe said to him, "You are right, Teacher; you have truly said that 'he is one, and besides him there is no other';* [33]*and 'to love him with all the heart, and with all the understanding, and with all the strength,' and 'to love one's neighbor as oneself,'—this is much more important than all whole burnt offerings and sacrifices."* [34]*When Jesus saw that he answered wisely, he said to him, "You are not far from the kingdom of God." After that no one dared to ask him any question.*

A scribe, a Jewish scholar of the Torah, asked Jesus a common question of the day, "Which commandment is the first of all?" (verse 28). This was a way of determining the central ideas of a rabbi's teaching. The commandments of the Torah were numerous; the rabbis would debate the distinctions between "heavy" and "light" commandments, and one count listed 248 positive and 365 negative commandments in the Torah. Rabbi Hillel, teaching a few decades before Jesus, was asked to teach the whole Torah while his student stood on one foot. Hillel replied, "What is hateful to you, do not to your neighbor: that is the whole Torah, while the rest is commentary."

When Jesus is asked what is the most important, he quotes two commandments from the Torah. The first is the Shema (Deut 6:4–5), the traditional prayer recited by Jews morning and evening. It affirms the oneness of God and that God must be loved totally and wholeheartedly. The second is the command to love one's neighbor: "You shall love your neighbor as yourself" (Lev 19:18). In combining these two, Jesus is saying that the essence of God's will for us is found in loving, and that practicing one of them without the other would be incomplete. By combining the second commandment with the first, and by prefacing them with the teaching on the oneness of God, Jesus thereby enlarges the definition of neighbor. If there is only one God who created all people, then every human being is our neighbor. Our love must be as broad as God's.

In the midst of the multitude of commands and precepts articulated through Israel's law, Jesus urges a singleness of purpose. Purity of heart that seeks only to love is the center around which all the many moral and legal practices of the law can be understood. Service of God must not be based on outward compulsion, but on the inner movement of the heart. The practice of love, as a grateful response to God's love for us, is the essence of the way of life that Jesus taught.

The scribe paraphrases what he has learned from Jesus, demonstrating that he has truly understood his words (verse 32–33). Then the scribe adds his own addendum: "This is much more important than all whole burnt offerings and sacrifices." The scribe is echoing the witness of many Hebrew prophets who affirm that religion cannot be only a matter of ritual and outward practice. The scribe, like the prophets before him, expresses the primacy of love and heartfelt devotion. Truly he has grasped what it means to live under the reign of God (verse 34).

Reflection and discussion

• Why does Jesus insist on the linkage between love of God and love of neighbor (1 John 4:20–21)? How do I experience this linkage?

• What can I do to deepen my experience of each kind of love—love of God, neighbor, and self?

• How broad is my heart? What is most difficult for me in accepting Jesus' global understanding of who is my neighbor?

Prayer

Lord of Love, you taught that wholehearted love of God and neighbor is the essence of God's will for us. Give me a singleness of heart so that everything that I do may be an expression of my love. Give me a bigger heart so that my loving will be a reflection of yours.

"But I say to you that listen, Love your enemies, do good to those who hate you, bless those who curse you, pray for those who abuse you." Luke 6:27

The Heart of Mercy

LUKE 6:27–36 ²⁷"*But I say to you that listen, Love your enemies, do good to those who hate you, *²⁸*bless those who curse you, pray for those who abuse you. *²⁹*If anyone strikes you on the cheek, offer the other also; and from anyone who takes away your coat do not withhold even your shirt. *³⁰*Give to everyone who begs from you; and if anyone takes away your goods, do not ask for them again. *³¹*Do to others as you would have them do to you.*

³²*"If you love those who love you, what credit is that to you? For even sinners love those who love them. *³³*If you do good to those who do good to you, what credit is that to you? For even sinners do the same. *³⁴*If you lend to those from whom you hope to receive, what credit is that to you? Even sinners lend to sinners, to receive as much again. *³⁵*But love your enemies, do good, and lend, expecting nothing in return. Your reward will be great, and you will be children of the Most High; for he is kind to the ungrateful and the wicked. *³⁶*Be merciful, just as your Father is merciful.*

The human heart that is formed in loving unity with the heart of Christ does not act according to the impulses of human instincts or the standards of the world. Jesus offers his hearers a new standard of conduct toward others, a response that goes above and beyond the minimalism of "tit for tat" behavior. The norm for Christians is an always-expanding heart.

Jesus teaches his followers not to retaliate, not to reciprocate, not to let their response be formed by those who would do them harm. In the face of mistreatment—hating, cursing, abusing, striking, and stealing—those who follow the way of Jesus should respond in the opposite direction—loving, blessing, praying, and giving (verses 27–30). They are not to react in kind or to passively whine, rather they are to take the initiative and respond according to the principles of love, forgiveness, and generosity.

The model for Christian behavior is ultimately the love of God. We must love not only those who love us; we must do good not only to those who do good to us; we must lend not only to those who will repay us (verses 32–34). God acts with love and generosity toward all, no matter what their response, and so must we (verse 35). God acts with kindness and mercy toward the ungrateful and the wicked. God does not act according to people's merits or give what people deserve. The "golden rule" of "do as you would want done" is not the ultimate norm, but rather, "do as God would do." Jesus wants our hearts to be formed after the pattern of our merciful Father.

Reflection and discussion

• Why do you suppose Jesus changed his command from "love your neighbor" to "love your enemies"? What justification for the change might Jesus offer?

• Are these teachings of Jesus realistic and practical, or is living with a heart of mercy an idealistic vision?

• In what way does the teaching of Jesus go beyond the reciprocity of the golden rule (verse 31)?

• In what way do these teachings of Jesus challenge me to change or expand my heart?

Prayer

God the Most High, you are good and merciful to those who love you and those who do not. You do not give me what I deserve, but you shower your blessings upon me. Help me to be merciful as you are merciful and form my heart in loving unity with the heart of your Son Jesus.

The good person out of the good treasure of the heart produces good; for it is out of the abundance of the heart that the mouth speaks. Luke 6:45

The Heart's Treasure

LUKE 6:43–45 ⁴³"No good tree bears bad fruit, nor again does a bad tree bear good fruit; ⁴⁴for each tree is known by its own fruit. Figs are not gathered from thorns, nor are grapes picked from a bramble bush. ⁴⁵The good person out of the good treasure of the heart produces good, and the evil person out of evil treasure produces evil; for it is out of the abundance of the heart that the mouth speaks.

LUKE 12:22–34 ²²He said to his disciples, "Therefore I tell you, do not worry about your life, what you will eat, or about your body, what you will wear. ²³For life is more than food, and the body more than clothing. ²⁴Consider the ravens: they neither sow nor reap, they have neither storehouse nor barn, and yet God feeds them. Of how much more value are you than the birds! ²⁵And can any of you by worrying add a single hour to your span of life? ²⁶If then you are not able to do so small a thing as that, why do you worry about the rest? ²⁷Consider the lilies, how they grow: they neither toil nor spin; yet I tell you, even Solomon in all his glory was not clothed like one of these. ²⁸But if God so clothes the grass of the field, which is alive today and tomorrow is thrown into the oven, how *much more will he clothe you—you of little faith!* [29] *And do not keep striving for what you are to eat and what you are to drink, and do not keep worrying.* [30] *For it is the nations of the world that strive after all these things, and your Father knows that you need them.* [31] *Instead, strive for his kingdom, and these things will be given to you as well.*

[32] *"Do not be afraid, little flock, for it is your Father's good pleasure to give you the kingdom.* [33] *Sell your possessions, and give alms. Make purses for yourselves that do not wear out, an unfailing treasure in heaven, where no thief comes near and no moth destroys.* [34] *For where your treasure is, there your heart will be also."*

In all of these sayings, Jesus focuses on the quality of the human heart. Since the heart is the person's core, the center from which all decisions and actions flow, the quality of a person's heart is most essential. What a person says and does flows from the inside, from the core. Just as good fruit comes only from a tree that is interiorly sound, so a person produces good "out of the good treasure of the heart" (6:45).

The concerns of a person's heart determine the quality of a person's life. When we spend our time worrying about the material things of life our hearts are expressing a preoccupation with the fleeting things of this life. Jesus said, "Where your treasure is, there your heart will be also" (12:34). We put our time, energy, and resources into those things we value, those things dear to our hearts. When we invest our resources in the things of God's kingdom—works of love, justice, generosity, and forgiveness—we know that our hearts are centered on the things of life that last forever.

It is really deep fear that stimulates the acquisitive instinct within us. Life seems so fragile and unpredictable that we feel the need for possessions to make life secure. Only the inner understanding that life is God's gift and that we can trust God to provide what we need relieves that fear and give us interior freedom (verse 32). The understanding that life cannot be secured by possessions and that it is outside our control helps us to trust God and orient our lives toward permanent values. We can learn lessons from the freedom of the birds and the beauty of the flowers. If God so graciously cares for them, how much more will God provide for us!

Because we have an eternal destiny, what we do has everlasting consequences. Generosity to others not only helps those who have to worry daily about what they are to eat and wear, but it also gives us spiritual freedom and forms our hearts for God's kingdom. Actions like selling our possessions and giving alms create the kind of treasure that cannot be stolen by a thief or destroyed by moths (verse 33). Concern for the things of God's kingdom forms our hearts and expresses an inner, personal core that is free for love.

Reflection and discussion

• How do I give my heart a checkup? What are the symptoms I should look for?

• What lessons do I need to learn from the birds and the flowers?

• What are my greatest fears? In what ways do those fears prevent me from living fully from the heart?

Prayer

Master Jesus, you teach me to trust in God who cares for me more than I can imagine. Calm my worries and soothe my fears so that my heart will be open to respond to the real priorities of life. Teach me to seek first the kingdom of God so that all else will be given to me as well.

They said to each other, "Were not our hearts burning within us while he was talking to us on the road, while he was opening the scriptures to us?"

Luke 24:32

Hearts Enflamed

LUKE 24:25–35 ²⁵ *Then Jesus said to them, "Oh, how foolish you are, and how slow of heart to believe all that the prophets have declared!* ²⁶ *Was it not necessary that the Messiah should suffer these things and then enter into his glory?"* ²⁷ *Then beginning with Moses and all the prophets, he interpreted to them the things about himself in all the Scriptures.*

²⁸ *As they came near the village to which they were going, he walked ahead as if he were going on.* ²⁹ *But they urged him strongly, saying, "Stay with us, because it is almost evening and the day is now nearly over." So he went in to stay with them.* ³⁰ *When he was at the table with them, he took bread, blessed and broke it, and gave it to them.* ³¹ *Then their eyes were opened, and they recognized him; and he vanished from their sight.* ³² *They said to each other, "Were not our hearts burning within us while he was talking to us on the road, while he was opening the scriptures to us?"* ³³ *That same hour they got up and returned to Jerusalem; and they found the eleven and their companions gathered together.* ³⁴ *They were saying, "The Lord has risen indeed, and he has appeared to Simon!"* ³⁵ *Then they told what had happened on the road, and how he had been made known to them in the breaking of the bread.*

The teaching of the risen Jesus about the Scriptures brought the two disciples from being "slow of heart" (verse 25) to the condition of "hearts burning" (verse 32). As they walked along the road toward Emmaus, Jesus gave them a lesson from the Hebrew Scriptures. He showed them how the writings of the Old Testament have come to their fulfillment in him: "Beginning with Moses and all the prophets, he interpreted to them the things about himself in all the Scriptures" (verse 27). At first, the disciples were "slow of heart" to believe; they were reluctant and unable to understand. To believe in Jesus, in the necessity of the Messiah's suffering and entry into glory (verse 26), requires a fuller understanding of the Scriptures. The ancient texts must be seen in the new light of God's messianic fulfillment and the resurrection of Christ.

Because Jesus had first interpreted the Scriptures for them, they were then able to recognize him "in the breaking of the bread" (verse 35). And having recognized the risen presence of Christ, they were then able to look back and realize that their hearts were "burning" while Jesus was "opening the Scriptures" (verse 32). The disciples experienced this new way of reading the ancient Scriptures given by the risen Jesus as a fire burning in their hearts. This experience of deep love and fiery enthusiasm would soon be unleashed with the coming of the Holy Spirit at Pentecost so that all people might experience their hearts aflame.

The metaphor of the burning heart refers to both the light and the heat that comes from a flame of fire. Since the heart is the center of a person's understanding and desire, the burning heart expresses the fact that the disciples received new insight and felt deep fervor that they could not contain. They immediately returned to Jerusalem to enthusiastically share their experience with others. They were bursting with desire to evangelize so that what filled their hearts could fill the hearts of others.

Reflection and discussion

• What was the process through which the risen Jesus transformed the hearts of his two disciples?

• What did the disciples mean when they described their hearts as burning? When have I experienced my heart burning in this way?

• The primary purpose of studying Scripture is not information but transformation. How can "opening the Scriptures" (verse 32) create a deeper, personal change in me?

• In what way does devotion to the Sacred Heart of Jesus impel a person toward the work of evangelization?

Prayer

Risen Lord, you make your presence known in word and sacrament. As I read your Scriptures and celebrate your Eucharist, open my eyes to your presence and enflame my heart with loving zeal for you.

But Mary treasured all these words and pondered them in her heart. Luke 2:19

The Holy Heart of Mary

LUKE 2:13–19, 33–35, 51–52 ¹³*And suddenly there was with the angel a multitude of the heavenly host, praising God and saying,* ¹⁴*"Glory to God in the highest heaven, and on earth peace among those whom he favors!"* ¹⁵*When the angels had left them and gone into heaven, the shepherds said to one another, "Let us go now to Bethlehem and see this thing that has taken place, which the Lord has made known to us."* ¹⁶*So they went with haste and found Mary and Joseph, and the child lying in the manger.* ¹⁷*When they saw this, they made known what had been told them about this child;* ¹⁸*and all who heard it were amazed at what the shepherds told them.* ¹⁹*But Mary treasured all these words and pondered them in her heart.*

³³*And the child's father and mother were amazed at what was being said about him.* ³⁴*Then Simeon blessed them and said to his mother Mary, "This child is destined for the falling and the rising of many in Israel, and to be a sign that will be opposed* ³⁵*so that the inner thoughts of many will be revealed—and a sword will pierce your own soul too."*

⁵¹*His mother treasured all these things in her heart.* ⁵²*And Jesus increased in wisdom and in years, and in divine and human favor.*

T he union of the hearts of Jesus and Mary began when the heart of Jesus developed in Mary's womb beneath her own heart. Jesus felt the heartbeat of Mary from the womb, and Mary felt the heartbeat of her son on her breast. Originating with the announcement of the angel and continuing until the end of time, the heart of Mary expresses her maternal love for her son and her wholehearted commitment to his saving mission.

Luke's gospel speaks explicitly about the heart of Mary in two texts from the accounts of Jesus' infancy and childhood. Concluding the narrative of Jesus' birth the gospel states, "Mary treasured all these words and pondered them in her heart" (verse 19), and concluding the childhood narrative of Jesus in the temple the gospel states, "His mother treasured all these things in her heart" (verse 51). Mary was beginning to fill her heart with a lifetime of experiences that would unite her intimately with the mission of her Son.

Mary was filled with grace and highly favored by God for her singular role as the mother of the Savior (1:28). Mary gave Jesus his humanity. With her husband, Joseph, Mary first taught Jesus how to pray and how to love. She was the first to discover the perfection of the heart of Jesus: his growing awareness of the Father, his obedient love, his passion for God's kingdom. It was Mary's privilege throughout her life to contemplate these divine mysteries in her heart.

Simeon, the aging prophet in Jerusalem's temple, foresaw the joint suffering of mother and child in the future mission of Israel's messiah. Predicting the opposition her son would face, he spoke also about the suffering of Mary herself: "And a sword will pierce your own soul too" (verse 35). Though Mary suffered the rejection of her son throughout his ministry, her pain was never so intense as at the cross. As the heart of Jesus was pierced with the lance, the soul of Mary was pierced with a sword of sorrow, expressing the profound, mystical union of the hearts of Jesus and Mary.

When Mary is mentioned for the last time in Luke's narrative, she is with the apostles, praying and waiting for the coming of the Holy Spirit at Pentecost (Acts 1:14). By depicting her on this first page of church history, Luke shows her to be at the heart of Christ's church. From her place in heaven, Mary remains the mother of Christ and the mother of all God's children. With Mary, the church will listen to God's word, ponder it with holy hearts, and empowered by the Holy Spirit, respond with joyful obedience and tender love.

Reflection and discussion

• What might be the most valuable treasures stored and pondered in the heart of Mary?

• For what reason is the heart of Mary honored in union with the sacred heart of Jesus?

• How can I love Jesus with the heart of Mary and love Mary with the heart of Jesus?

Prayer

Glorified Lord, through the loving heart of Mary, teach me to treasure your word and ponder it in my heart. Send your Holy Spirit to enflame my heart so that my life may brighten and warm the lives of those around me.

SUGGESTIONS FOR FACILITATORS, GROUP SESSION 5

1. Welcome group members and ask if anyone has any questions, announcements, or requests.

2. You may want to pray this prayer as a group:

Holy Wisdom, you invite us to come to you, to learn from you, and find rest for our souls. Give us the gentleness, humility, and simplicity of your heart. Expand our hearts so that we can choose the way of generosity and forgiveness over resentment and revenge. Calm our fears and insecurities, so that we may quit grasping at things and keep trusting in you. Send your Holy Spirit upon us to set our hearts aflame with understanding and zeal. May we treasure and ponder your word in imitation of Mary, our mother.

3. Ask one or more of the following questions:
   - What most intrigued you from this week's study?
   - What makes you want to know and understand more of God's word?

4. Discuss lessons 19 through 24. Choose one or more of the questions for reflection and discussion from each lesson to talk over as a group.

5. Ask the group members to name one thing they have most appreciated about the way the group has worked during this Bible study. Ask group members to discuss any changes they might suggest in the way the group works in future studies.

6. Invite group members to complete lessons 25 through 30 on their own during the six days before the next meeting. They should write out their own answers to the questions as preparation for next week's session.

7. Discuss images of the Sacred Heart and what the Scriptures tell us about the meaning of those images.

8. Conclude by praying aloud together the prayer at the end of one of the lessons discussed. You may want to conclude the prayer by asking members to voice prayers of thanksgiving.

Hope does not disappoint us, because God's love has been poured into our hearts through the Holy Spirit that has been given to us. Rom 5:5

God's Love Poured into Our Hearts

ROMANS 5:1–11 ¹*Therefore, since we are justified by faith, we have peace with God through our Lord Jesus Christ, ²through whom we have obtained access to this grace in which we stand; and we boast in our hope of sharing the glory of God. ³And not only that, but we also boast in our sufferings, knowing that suffering produces endurance, ⁴and endurance produces character, and character produces hope, ⁵and hope does not disappoint us, because God's love has been poured into our hearts through the Holy Spirit that has been given to us.*

⁶For while we were still weak, at the right time Christ died for the ungodly. ⁷Indeed, rarely will anyone die for a righteous person—though perhaps for a good person someone might actually dare to die. ⁸But God proves his love for us in that while we still were sinners Christ died for us. ⁹Much more surely then, now that we have been justified by his blood, will we be saved through him from the wrath of God. ¹⁰For if while we were enemies, we were reconciled to God through the death of his Son, much more surely, having been reconciled, will we be saved by his life. ¹¹But more than that, we even boast in God through our Lord Jesus Christ, through whom we have now received reconciliation.

In this triumphant text Paul summarizes the divine process that leads to our salvation. The process of God's action on our behalf is rooted in God's love for us. In a way unparalleled by human love, God has given himself to us without restraint: "God's love has been poured into our hearts" (verse 5). The human heart is the vessel for divine love surging into our lives. The image is that of life-giving water being poured on a thirsty land (Isa 44:3), torrential rains in an arid desert. God's love gushes forth into our hearts with abandon by the Holy Spirit.

It is impossible for us to understand the dimensions of divine love, but we can see the manifestation of God's love in the death of Christ for us: "God proves his love for us in that while we were sinners Christ died for us" (verse 8). The act is humanly inconceivable and contrary to all expectations (verse 7). God's love (*agape* in Greek) is unconditional love, independent of any worthiness or merit on the part of the recipient. This love, supremely expressed in the death of Christ on our behalf, is the design for the whole Christian life. We can love others because "he first loved us" (1 John 4:19). We are called to love in the way that God loves, not because of expected return but in spite of the fact that the other has done nothing to merit that love (Luke 6:32–36).

When we accept the redeeming death of Christ through our response in faith, we are "justified" and "reconciled" to God. Both words refer to the restoration of our relationship with God that had been lost through sin. The results of this access to God's grace that we have received from Christ are "peace" and "hope" (verse 1–2). Peace is the foretaste of the fullness of salvation that we await; hope is the confident expectation that we will share fully in the glory of God. God's grace is strong enough to give us peace and hope even in the midst of suffering (verses 3–4). When our lives are united with Christ, affliction aids the work of grace within us and prepares us for the glory to come.

When God's love has been poured into our hearts by the Holy Spirit, we are filled with the gifts of peace and hope. We know in our hearts that we will experience the fullness of salvation that God has assured us through the redeeming death of his Son. We trust God completely to finish the work of our salvation and bring us to the glory he has promised.

Reflection and discussion

• In what way does God "prove" his love for us? Why is this such a convincing proof?

• How would I describe the peace and hope that I experience as a result of God's grace at work within me?

• Is confidence in the future a characteristic of my life? For what reasons does Paul say we can be confident in God's plans for us?

Prayer

Lord Jesus Christ, you died for us while we were still sinners as the clear proof of God's unconditional love. Help me to open my heart through faith so that the Holy Spirit may fill it with divine love, and give me confidence in the glory of God to come.

Who will separate us from the love of Christ? Will hardship, or distress, or persecution, or famine, or nakedness, or peril, or sword? Rom 8:35

Knowing God's Love in Christ Jesus

ROMANS 8:31–39 *[31]What then are we to say about these things? If God is for us, who is against us? [32]He who did not withhold his own Son, but gave him up for all of us, will he not with him also give us everything else? [33]Who will bring any charge against God's elect? It is God who justifies. [34]Who is to condemn? It is Christ Jesus, who died, yes, who was raised, who is at the right hand of God, who indeed intercedes for us. [35]Who will separate us from the love of Christ? Will hardship, or distress, or persecution, or famine, or nakedness, or peril, or sword? [36]As it is written,*

> *"For your sake we are being killed all day long;*
> *we are accounted as sheep to be slaughtered."*

[37]No, in all these things we are more than conquerors through him who loved us. [38]For I am convinced that neither death, nor life, nor angels, nor rulers, nor things present, nor things to come, nor powers, [39]nor height, nor depth, nor anything else in all creation, will be able to separate us from the love of God in Christ Jesus our Lord.

The "love of God" that has been poured out "in Christ Jesus our Lord" is the foundation of Christian life and hope (verse 39). What Jesus has done for humanity is the visible and certain manifestation of God's love. Absolutely nothing can disturb that unshakable foundation. In this jubilant hymn of praise to God's love, Paul sings of the victory that God has gained for humanity over all powers that might conceivably oppose that love.

"God is for us" (verse 31)—this is the essence of the gospel Paul proclaims. As with all great truths, its articulation is disarmingly simple. With elevated eloquence Paul praises God for his absolute faithfulness verified for the world in the person of Jesus Christ "who died, who was raised, who is at the right hand of God, who indeed intercedes for us" (verse 34). As the one who died, Jesus redeemed humanity from sin and judgment; as the one who was raised, he assures us of victory over death and the gift of eternal life. As the one at the right hand of God, Jesus reigns as Lord in power and glory. As the one who intercedes for us, the enthroned Lord exercises his authority on our behalf. Jesus assures us that God is for us, not only in his sacrificial love on the cross, but now in his sustaining love as our glorious Lord.

The faithfulness of God's love is extolled through six rhetorical questions. The questions answer themselves and praise the God who is always for us. With God on our side the forces that are marshaled against us cannot prevail. Since God even gave up his Son for our sake, paying the highest price, we can certainly trust God to give us everything we could possibly need (verse 32). Because the only one of any significance who could bring a charge against us or condemn us is the one who has done everything for us, then truly we have nothing to be afraid of (verses 33–34). Since God has proved his love for us absolutely, we need not worry about any opposition.

Not even the greatest dangers and most painful experiences that humans could undergo can separate us from God's love (verses 35–36). Since God has made us "more than conquerors" (verse 37), having conquered the greatest of all enemies through Christ, then we can live with absolute confidence that God is for us. Not even the strongest forces of the universe—earthly or cosmic, natural or supernatural, present or future—can separate us from God's love (verses 38–39). Paul has used all the fiercest terms he could imagine to show how ineradicable is the divine love which he has come to know through Jesus Christ.

Reflection and discussion

• Which of the threats of verses 35 and 38 are most real to me? Why can they not separate me from God's love?

• Why can "God is for us" be described as the gospel in a nutshell? What practical implications do these words have for me?

• Do I really trust God in all things? What parts of this hymn help bolster my trust?

Prayer

Lord Jesus Christ, you reign in glory over all the powers of the world. Through your death and resurrection you have demonstrated the trustworthiness and fidelity of God's love. In the face of life's trials and tragedies assure me that nothing can separate me from that love.

If you confess with your lips that Jesus is Lord and believe in your heart that God raised him from the dead, you will be saved. Rom 10:9

Believing in Your Heart

ROMANS 10:1–13 ¹*Brothers and sisters, my heart's desire and prayer to God for [the Israelites] is that they may be saved.* ²*I can testify that they have a zeal for God, but it is not enlightened.* ³*For, being ignorant of the righteousness that comes from God, and seeking to establish their own, they have not submitted to God's righteousness.* ⁴*For Christ is the end of the law so that there may be righteousness for everyone who believes.*

⁵*Moses writes concerning the righteousness that comes from the law, that "the person who does these things will live by them."* ⁶*But the righteousness that comes from faith says, "Do not say in your heart, 'Who will ascend into heaven?'" (that is, to bring Christ down)* ⁷*"or 'Who will descend into the abyss?'" (that is, to bring Christ up from the dead).* ⁸*But what does it say?*

"The word is near you,
on your lips and in your heart"

(that is, the word of faith that we proclaim); ⁹*because if you confess with your lips that Jesus is Lord and believe in your heart that God raised him from the dead, you will be saved.* ¹⁰*For one believes with the heart and so is justified, and one confesses with the mouth and so is saved.* ¹¹*The scripture says, "No one who believes in him will be put to shame."* ¹²*For there is no distinction between Jew and Greek; the same Lord is Lord of all and is generous to all who call on him.* ¹³*For, "Everyone who calls on the name of the Lord shall be saved."*

Christianity, like the faith of ancient Israel, is primarily a religion of the heart. A trusting relationship with God at the core of one's being is the essence of what God wants from his people. The ancient Torah told Israel that the inexplicable love of God for them was the foundation of God's saving relationship with them. God "set his heart" on Israel (Deut 7:7), not because of anything they had done, but simply because he desired to love them. The gospel of Jesus Christ tells us that God so loved the world that he sent his Son as the way to life for us. The salvation that God offers to us through Christ is not something that we can merit or earn; it is pure grace, the gift of God to his people because he loves us.

Israel was called to accept the life God offered to them through a heartfelt response to God shaped by the covenant. The Torah made it clear that they never merited God's gifts; but they could refuse them through disobeying the covenant. Only Israel's Messiah truly responded to God through heartfelt obedience to the Torah. On his heart the Torah is written, and in his heart the new covenant has come to Israel (Jer 31:33). In his heart is the first and perfect realization of the new covenant. In this way, as Paul says, "Christ is the end of the law" (verse 4). He does not replace the law or end its value, but he is the final goal of the law. The purpose for which the Torah was established, complete trust in God, is fulfilled in Christ.

As the ultimate goal of the Torah, Christ is now the basis for trusting God. The Torah has now been embodied—incarnated—in Christ. As the new Torah, Christ has brought God's history of salvation with Israel to its culmination. Paul can therefore interpret the words of Deuteronomy in light of Christ. God's will for us is not something that we have to go up to heaven or down into the abyss to find (verses 6–7), for God has already brought Christ down from heaven (in the incarnation) and brought Christ up from the abyss of death (in the resurrection). Rather, we have only to accept in faith what God has already done for us: "The word is near you, on your lips and in your heart" (verse 8; Deut 30:12–14).

Trusting God totally "with your heart" and acknowledging that trust "with your lips" is the way to salvation (verse 9). Because Jesus fulfilled God's will so perfectly and brought God's law to its completion, with his heart and his lips, our relationship to him in faith is the way we experience the goal of the Torah. Everyone who believes and confesses that Jesus is Lord and that God raised him from the dead will be saved. We cannot earn or merit God's gift of grace; we receive the "righteousness that comes from faith" (verse 6), a trusting acceptance of the gift God has given us.

Reflection and discussion

• In what ways does Paul describe Christianity as a religion of the heart? In what way was the religion of ancient Israel also a religion of the heart?

• In what way does Christ completely fulfill and embody the Torah?

• Why is it so tempting to think that I can earn God's gifts of grace? Why is it so difficult to trust God completely?

Prayer

Christ Jesus, by your complete trust in God, you have fulfilled the goal of the covenant. In your incarnation and resurrection God has brought you near to us. Give me your heart so that I can trust God completely and surrender my life to his will.

I pray that you may have the power to comprehend, with all the saints, what is the breadth and length and height and depth, and to know the love of Christ that surpasses knowledge. Eph 3:18–19

That Christ May Dwell in Your Hearts

EPHESIANS 3:7–21 *⁷Of this gospel I have become a servant according to the gift of God's grace that was given me by the working of his power. ⁸Although I am the very least of all the saints, this grace was given to me to bring to the Gentiles the news of the boundless riches of Christ, ⁹and to make everyone see what is the plan of the mystery hidden for ages in God who created all things; ¹⁰so that through the church the wisdom of God in its rich variety might now be made known to the rulers and authorities in the heavenly places. ¹¹This was in accordance with the eternal purpose that he has carried out in Christ Jesus our Lord, ¹²in whom we have access to God in boldness and confidence through faith in him. ¹³I pray therefore that you may not lose heart over my sufferings for you; they are your glory.*

¹⁴For this reason I bow my knees before the Father, ¹⁵from whom every family in heaven and on earth takes its name. ¹⁶I pray that, according to the riches of his glory, he may grant that you may be strengthened in your inner being with power through his Spirit, ¹⁷and that Christ may dwell in your hearts through faith, as you are being rooted and grounded in love. ¹⁸I pray that you may have the power to comprehend, with all the saints, what is the breadth and length and height and depth, ¹⁹and to know the love of Christ that surpasses knowledge, so that you may be filled with all the fullness of God.

²⁰Now to him who by the power at work within us is able to accomplish abundantly far more than all we can ask or imagine, ²¹to him be glory in the church and in Christ Jesus to all generations, forever and ever. Amen.

Paul's heart overflowed with amazement and gratitude for the ways God's grace had worked in him (verse 7). Through God's grace he was chosen to bring to all people—Jews and Gentiles alike—news of the "boundless riches of Christ" (verse 8). By penetrating more and more deeply into the heart of Christ, the believer discovers vast riches, a treasury that is endless and even beyond comprehension. God's revelation of salvation in Christ is "the mystery hidden for ages" (verse 9); it is "the wisdom of God" that is now made known through the church (verse10). Through our union with Christ in faith, all barriers have been removed that would prevent us from approaching God openly and confidently (verse 12).

Paul's amazement at what God has done in revealing Christ's salvation to the world moves him to humbly kneel before the Father of all and pray for the church (verse 14). Drawing upon the vast reservoir of God's riches, Paul prays that God will strengthen the "inner being" of his readers through the power of God's Spirit (verse 16), and that Christ will dwell in their hearts through faith (verse 17). The "heart" and the "inner being" describe the deepest identity of the believer. The abiding presence of Christ in the believer's heart and the power of the Holy Spirit working within are two ways of describing how God works in the believer's life.

When Christ dwells within the human heart, the believer is "rooted and grounded in love" (verse 17). Paul uses both a botanical and an architectural metaphor to describe this life empowered by the Holy Spirit. Love is the rich soil in which the roots of our lives grow; love is the firm foundation on which the structure of our lives is built. Paul prays that his readers will have the ability to comprehend how wide and long and high and deep is "the love of Christ" (verses 18–19). There is no way to describe the magnitude of Christ's love. This love which suffuses the vastness of creation is the same love that penetrates the boundless depths of the human heart. No matter how much power we have to understand, all of our efforts fail to comprehend "the love of Christ that surpasses knowledge." The more deeply we penetrate the heart of Christ, the more we discover the vast treasury of love that is beyond comprehension.

Paul's desire for his readers ultimately is that they be "filled with all the fullness of God" (verse 19). The more we are united with the heart of Christ, allowing God's Spirit to work in our deepest center, the more God's divine life fills our own. If we really "know" this divine love in the biblical sense of having direct experience of it, then we cannot but be filled with the fullness of God who is love.

Reflection and discussion

• What have I discovered of the "boundless riches of Christ" (verse 8)? Why is it impossible to understand or comprehend the love of Christ (verse 19)?

• What is the relationship of the Father, Son, and Holy Spirit to my human heart (verses 14–17)?

• How is the dwelling of Christ in our hearts (verse 17) the way to be filled with God's fullness (verse 19)? In what way have I experienced this grace of God in my own life?

• Visualize Christ revealing his heart and reaching out to the world. How does this image help me to comprehend "the breadth and length and height and depth" of Christ's love?

• Which phrase of Paul's prayer do I want to remember today? Why is it particularly meaningful to me?

Prayer

Christ Jesus our Lord, no words can express the limitless riches that fill your heart. Help me to glimpse the breadth and length, the height and depth of your love. I pray that your love which fills the universe may penetrate my heart and transform my life.

In this is love, not that we loved God but that he loved us and sent his Son to be the atoning sacrifice for our sins. 1 John 4:10

Love in Truth and Action

1 JOHN 3:16–24 [16] *We know love by this, that he laid down his life for us— and we ought to lay down our lives for one another.* [17] *How does God's love abide in anyone who has the world's goods and sees a brother or sister in need and yet refuses help?*

[18] *Little children, let us love, not in word or speech, but in truth and action.* [19] *And by this we will know that we are from the truth and will reassure our hearts before him* [20] *whenever our hearts condemn us; for God is greater than our hearts, and he knows everything.* [21] *Beloved, if our hearts do not condemn us, we have boldness before God;* [22] *and we receive from him whatever we ask, because we obey his commandments and do what pleases him.*

[23] *And this is his commandment, that we should believe in the name of his Son Jesus Christ and love one another, just as he has commanded us.* [24] *All who obey his commandments abide in him, and he abides in them. And by this we know that he abides in us, by the Spirit that he has given us.*

1 JOHN 4:7–16 [7] *Beloved, let us love one another, because love is from God; everyone who loves is born of God and knows God.* [8] *Whoever does not love does* *not know God, for God is love. ⁹God's love was revealed among us in this way: God sent his only Son into the world so that we might live through him. ¹⁰In this is love, not that we loved God but that he loved us and sent his Son to be the atoning sacrifice for our sins. ¹¹Beloved, since God loved us so much, we also ought to love one another. ¹²No one has ever seen God; if we love one another, God lives in us, and his love is perfected in us.*

¹³By this we know that we abide in him and he in us, because he has given us of his Spirit. ¹⁴And we have seen and do testify that the Father has sent his Son as the Savior of the world. ¹⁵God abides in those who confess that Jesus is the Son of God, and they abide in God. ¹⁶So we have known and believe the love that God has for us.

God is love, and those who abide in love abide in God, and God abides in them.

If love is genuine, it must be visible and active, not just a matter of "word or speech" but of "truth and action" (3:18). Jesus willingly laying down his life for us is the decisive evidence of authentic love. We demonstrate this love when we, in turn, lay down our lives for one another (3:16). But we deny this love when we fail to help our brothers and sisters in need (3:17). Real love is a personal commitment to give oneself for the highest good of another. It has a sacrificial element and can be tested by whether or not it is made evident through practical action.

Our relationship with God is always centered in the heart. It is expressed in the two-fold commandment: "Believe in the name of his Son" and "love one another" (3:23). Faith in Christ is a heart-centered commitment of our whole self in response to God's revelation in Christ; love is an inner response to others in imitation of the love God has shown to us. Our hearts will be reassured when we are in a confident relationship with the One who knows us completely, because "God is greater than our hearts" (3:19–21). With this heart-to-heart relationship with God, we know that God abides in us and we abide in him (3:24; 4:16).

God's love is the source of all other expressions of love. If fact, God's essential nature is love, for "God is love" (4:8, 16). Because love has its origin in God, "everyone who loves is born of God and knows God" (4:7). The love we show to others is proof of the fact that we have been "born from above" or "born of water and Spirit" (John 3:3, 5, 7). Authentic love is expressed among those who have come to know God's love through Jesus Christ, making them members of God's family so that they know God in a personal and intimate way.

The God who is love reveals that love in concrete, historical events—in sending his only Son into the world and, supremely, in his atoning sacrifice for our sins (4:9–10). This is the definitive expression of love, the true standard of authentic love. This love that God has shown us becomes our mandate to love in this same way: "Since God loved us so much, we ought to love one another" (4:11). Our loving becomes, then, the means God uses to live in us and to perfect his life within us (4:12). Even though "no one has ever seen God," God's presence can be felt and truly experienced at work within the world when we love one another.

Reflection and discussion

• Why is it necessary for human beings to receive love before they are able to give love? How does my experience prove this to be the case?

• How does the assurance of God's love give me the confidence and trust necessary to love and be loved?

• Why is the two-fold commandment—to believe in Christ and to love one another (3:23)—so necessary for a heart-to-heart relationship with God?

• What are the characteristics of genuine, authentic love? How do I know whether or not love is real?

• What is most difficult about this teaching for me? In what aspects of my life is this love most difficult to make concrete and real?

Prayer

Lord Jesus, you came into the world and gave your life for us to show the love of the Father's heart. Purify the love of my heart and make it like your own. Help me show to others the love that you have first shown to me.

This is the one who came by water and blood, Jesus Christ, not with the water only but with the water and the blood. And the Spirit is the one that testifies, for the Spirit is the truth. 1 John 5:6

The Spirit, the Water, and the Blood

1 JOHN 5:6–15 *⁶This is the one who came by water and blood, Jesus Christ, not with the water only but with the water and the blood. And the Spirit is the one that testifies, for the Spirit is the truth. ⁷There are three that testify: ⁸the Spirit and the water and the blood, and these three agree. ⁹If we receive human testimony, the testimony of God is greater; for this is the testimony of God that he has testified to his Son. ¹⁰Those who believe in the Son of God have the testimony in their hearts. Those who do not believe in God have made him a liar by not believing in the testimony that God has given concerning his Son. ¹¹And this is the testimony: God gave us eternal life, and this life is in his Son. ¹²Whoever has the Son has life; whoever does not have the Son of God does not have life.*

¹³I write these things to you who believe in the name of the Son of God, so that you may know that you have eternal life.

¹⁴And this is the boldness we have in him, that if we ask anything according to his will, he hears us. ¹⁵And if we know that he hears us in whatever we ask, we know that we have obtained the requests made of him.

The opponents of the community John addressed in his letter did not believe that the divine Christ could be truly human, nor that he could actually suffer and die. Furthermore, these opponents did not accept the sacrificial value of the cross or the saving significance of Christ's death. John's gospel had expressed the rich consequences of Christ's death by witnessing to the blood and the water that flowed from Christ's pierced side (John 19:34). For this reason, John emphatically affirms in his letter that Jesus Christ came "not with the water only but with water and the blood" (verse 6). Not only is Jesus the source of living water, as demonstrated throughout his life, he is also the redemptive sacrifice whose blood was poured out for us in his death.

At the cross, the beloved disciple saw the blood and water come from the side of Christ and "testified" to it (John 19:35). In the believing community, the Spirit continues to "testify," because "the Spirit is the truth" (verse 6). In fact, "there are three that testify: the Spirit and the water and the blood" (verses 7–8). The Spirit of truth that filled Jesus throughout his life is present with Christ's church, and it is through the Spirit that the church recognizes and understands the fullness of truth about Jesus.

The testimony offered by the Spirit, the water, and the blood is this: "God gave us eternal life, and this life is in his Son" (verse 11). This testimony of the Holy Spirit must become an internal testimony within each believer, "testimony in their hearts" (verse 10). Through the gift of faith, to all those "who believe in the Son of God," the Holy Spirit gives an inner confidence and assurance that Jesus Christ is trustworthy and worth the commitment of their lives.

Jesus Christ, from whose side blood and water poured at the cross, is risen and glorified. Yet, he still dispenses the blood and the water from his glorious side. He continues to give his church all the grace necessary so that believers can experience eternal life. These writings of John's community emphasize that eternal life is a present spiritual reality (verse 13), the qualitatively different life present in those who believe in Jesus and receive the graces that flow from his heart. With confident faith we know that whatever we ask that is God's will for us, God will hear us and grant what we need (verses 14–15). This life of faith centered on the Sacred Heart of Jesus gives us a deep trust. It offers us everything that we need and so enables us to share the love that we have known in Christ with the world in which we live.

Reflection and discussion

• What do the Spirit, the water, and the blood reveal to us about Jesus?

• How do I let the testimony offered by the Spirit, the water, and the blood become an internal testimony in my heart?

• In what way is eternal life a present reality for me? How can baptism and Eucharist become deeper sources of God's life within me?

Prayer

Glorious Lord, at your death on the cross, you poured out upon your church the saving water of life and the redemptive blood of your sacrifice. From your pierced and glorified heart, give me the grace of eternal life and grant me all the blessings I need to live my life according to your loving will.

SUGGESTIONS FOR FACILITATORS, GROUP SESSION 6

1. Welcome group members and make any final announcements or requests.

2. You may want to pray this prayer as a group:

Lord Jesus Christ, you have poured divine love into our hearts through the Holy Spirit. We know that absolutely nothing has the power to separate us from that love. You gave us the testimony of the Spirit, the water, and the blood for our eternal life. As we penetrate ever more deeply into the boundless riches of your Sacred Heart, help us to glimpse the magnitude of your love that fills the universe. As we study the Scriptures, give us the grace to believe in our hearts and to love others in truth and action.

3. Ask one or more of the following questions:
   - How has this study of the Sacred Heart helped your life in Christ?
   - In what way has this study challenged you the most?

4. Discuss lessons 25 through 30. Choose one or more of the questions for reflection and discussion from each lesson to discuss as a group.

5. Ask the group if they would like to study another in the Threshold Bible Study series. Discuss the topic and dates, and make a decision among those interested. Ask the group members to suggest people they would like to invite to participate in the next study series.

6. Ask the group to discuss the insights that stand out most from this study over the past six weeks.

7. Conclude by praying aloud the following prayer or another of your own choosing:

Holy Spirit of the living God, you inspired the writers of the Scriptures and you have guided our study during these weeks. Continue to deepen our love for the word of God in the holy Scriptures and draw us more deeply into the heart of Jesus. We thank you for the confident hope you have given us through the love of the Sacred Heart. Through this study, lead us to worship and witness more fully and fervently, and bless us now and always with the fire of your love.

Ordering Additional Studies

Available Threshold Titles

Eucharist

Angels of God

Pilgrimage in the Footsteps of Jesus

Jerusalem, the Holy City

The Names of Jesus

Advent Light

The Tragic and Triumphant Cross

People of the Passion

The Resurrection and the Life

Mysteries of the Rosary

The Lamb and the Beasts

The Feasts of Judaism

The Sacred Heart of Jesus

The Holy Spirit and Spiritual Gifts

Stewardship of the Earth

For a complete description of these and upcoming titles, visit our website at www.ThresholdBibleStudy.com.

For information or orders, visit www.23rdpublications.com or call us at 1-800-321-0411.

Threshold Bible Study is available through your local bookstore or directly from the publisher. The following volume discounts are available from the publisher:

$12.95 (1-3 copies)

$11.95 (4-7 copies)

$10.95 (8-11 copies)

$9.95 (12 or more copies)